# On Common Ground

# On Common Ground
## A Programme for Teaching Poetry

*Jill Pirrie*

Illustrated by Eileen Hogan

HODDER AND STOUGHTON
LONDON   SYDNEY   AUCKLAND   TORONTO

*To My Mother and Father*

'The world is troubled
With a lack of looking.'
*George Tardios*

ISBN 0 340 41653 X

First published 1987

Copyright © 1987 Jill Pirrie

Foreword © 1987 Ted Hughes

Typeset in Monotype Baskerville by Cotswold Typesetting Limited, Gloucester.
Printed in Great Britain for Hodder and Stoughton Educational, a division of Hodder and Stoughton Ltd, Mill Road, Dunton Green, Sevenoaks, Kent, by St Edmundsbury Press Limited, Bury St Edmunds, Suffolk.

# Contents

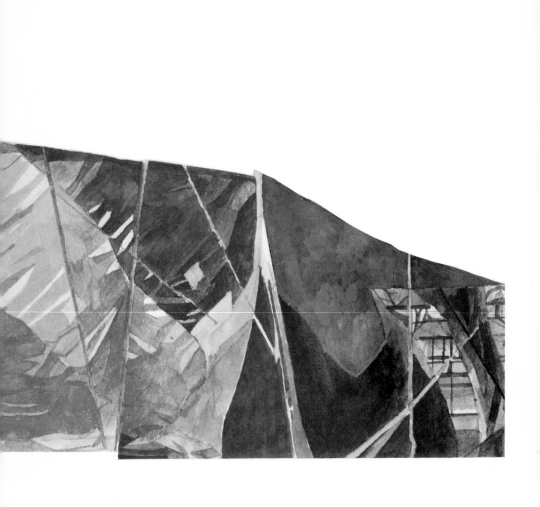

# Foreword

For readers not fully aware of Jill Pirrie's extraordinary success in the teaching of written English at Halesworth Middle School in Suffolk, perhaps the following anecdote will give some notion of it.

In the latest (1987) W. H. Smith Young Writers' Competition, her pupils were represented by about 60 names. This in itself is an unusually massive block entry. The total intake, from schools all over the country, was just under 40,000, with the main bulk of this number falling within the two upper age categories. In these two categories, the Competition offers 40 prizes. And of these 40 prizes, Halesworth Middle School took ten. In other words, Jill Pirrie's pupils carried off 25% of the prizes for the entire country.

This is by no means the whole story. Of the remaining Halesworth entries, 50 received Commendation Awards. This division of ten prizes and 50 Commendation Awards, out of about 60 entries, conceals something even more remarkable, which confronted the judges as a problem.

For the judges this problem was an immediate, practical one – how to fit the volume of Halesworth's achievement into a competition that had never encountered anything like it; but it anticipates, I think, the much bigger question which Jill Pirrie's example now poses to English teaching in particular and perhaps to education in general.

To understand this question, one needs to know something of how schools normally perform in these prizewinning events. At the moment, children's writing competitions constitute the only national survey of what is being accomplished by pupils and teachers in this field. Among the current competitions, perhaps the W. H. Smith Young Writers' Competition, mentioned above, gives the best idea, since its annual archives go back nearly 30 years, with some of the judges (myself included) having served for most of that time.

Each year, as we read through the dizzying medley of entries, we are aware of two kinds of outstanding talent. The first kind, what might be called the old-fashioned kind, appears as a gifted young writer emerging alone, perhaps very young, with a couple of inspired pages, from his or her school. It happens that often enough we never hear from this writer again. Or, maybe, the same name and talent reappears for two or three years – then vanishes. One can't help wondering what influences are operating here. Did the pupil meet, briefly, a special teacher? Or was it pure, natural talent flaring out against the odds before being snuffed?

The second kind of talent arrives always as one of a group of gifted entries from a particular school. This is a regular phenomenon, and there have been memorable cases. A school will submit half a dozen or perhaps more entries, all of them outstanding in some arresting way, with one of them, maybe (and maybe more) evoking the judges' response 'genius'. The following year, the same school does it again, but with a new name or two in among. This can go on for several years: always the same wealth of talent from the same school, but with odd names changing each year. In any given year, two or three schools might be producing perennial fugues of this kind. Here, obviously, what we are observing is not pure, natural talent flaring out against the odds, but 'latent' talent being unearthed, in an average class, from ordinary pupils – by a particular teacher.

It is a controlled experiment of a sort. When, as usually happens sooner or later, the supply from one of these notable schools suddenly dries up, how do we explain it? Where has all that flow of undoubted and prizewinning talent from that hitherto reliable source gone? And, of course, the simple answer is that the teacher has left.

We find nothing surprising about this, and yet, perhaps, it deserves more attention. In most academic subjects, the achievements of a class can generally be related closely to the skill of a teacher. But it is almost a truism to say that 'gifted writing' springs from outside the routine of 'academic subjects', and that the talent for it is either evident and innate or absent, either there or not there. Most of us share this belief: enough of us have classroom experience to support it: the untalented 99.9% balance the rare natural gift.

On the other hand, as we can see, the experience of the teachers behind these outstanding block entries is quite different. Their results directly contradict that common belief. And when you see them producing their golden crop year after year, from every type of school, against an assortment of cultural backgrounds, you begin to realise that these teachers don't need pupils with an 'evident, natural gift'. All they need is ordinary pupils. And in a good proportion of these pupils they will locate, and release, somehow, 'latent' talent, often enough exceptional talent.

The rumour that this small miracle will persist in happening lives uneasily alongside our conviction that it can't really be possible, and that it is 'unnatural'. The issues, after all, are uncertain, blurred by subjective opinion. And the whole business is closed in obscurity by one simple fact: the only people who actually see and compare all the evidence are a few judges on a competition. Even where the evidence leaks out, it is easily challenged by a politically respectable argument, which questions the concept of 'ordinary'. The sceptic suggests that these 'ordinary' pupils are not quite 'ordinary', and that apparently-ordinary pupils can respond so richly to a skilled teacher only because they are, in fact, helped by 'hidden advantages'. The implication is, as a rule, that these 'hidden advantages' are social ones, which set their lucky beneficiaries out of the ordinary.

In other areas of academic endeavour, fortunate background can obviously make a big difference. But when we are speaking of the mind's secret, creative activity, who knows what works as 'advantage' and what as 'disadvantage'? If historical precedent were anything to go by, we would have to say that creative talent seems to thrive best of all on what most of us would call 'disadvantage'. The right disadvantage can be a mighty spur to galvanise primal resources. And as with other uncanny proofs of ingenuity or energy, luminous verbal talent is a matter of galvanised resources. Maybe creative talent (creative talent of any kind) is just that: the conversion of disadvantages to their opposite, with the complication that none but the owner can know what registers, in secret, as a 'disadvantage'. (And perhaps we should add: with the proviso that all creative talent, which is always 'latent' to begin with, needs its special opportunity if it is to emerge.) From this point of view, we should give every child, in every school, the benefit of the doubt, as a dark horse.

This is where we see the relevance of Jill Pirrie's example; where her example becomes, as it were, trebly useful. Firstly, her Halesworth pupils are ideally average and 'ordinary', in the sense that they come from the whole range of backgrounds provided by a country town in Suffolk, and enjoy no specialised milieu of intellectual or literary or artistic sophistication. Secondly, her conversion rate, from ordinary pupil to remarkably talented and inventive young writer, is so phenomenally high – away beyond anything that has ever appeared before in the W. H. Smith Young Writers' Competition. And therefore, and finally, like nobody else, her example raises this almost alarming question: if 'latent' talent really is so plentiful, so much more abundant than had ever been guessed, what can be done about it? What can be done with this revelation of the unsuspected resources of the average, ordinary pupil? And she raises the other question, twin to this one and just as disturbing: are conventional educational methods out of phase with real human abilities?

This last question might seem rather sweeping. With Halesworth's 1987 entry the judges of the W. H. Smith Competition were forced to consider it. Some years ago we became aware that an outstanding teacher was at work in Halesworth. But, as I said earlier, this year her pupils became a problem.

The phalanx of 60 entries, which came through into the finals, made such an impact that our first reaction, defensive, was to debate whether we ought not to regard them as a category on their own, a class apart. This illustrates what I mean by Jill Pirrie's results being out of phase with those produced by more conventional teaching methods. We simply found it very difficult to appraise the work of her pupils using the criteria we had developed for all the others. Not that the best of hers were immeasurably better than the best from other schools. But *so many* of her pupils had written *so much* that was astonishingly good, that they affected our judging procedure. To a degree, and in a very substantial way (and this again touches the deeper, wider educational 'problem'), they radically changed our idea of what an ordinary pupil can be expected to do. It was only by fighting especially hard for the best entries from other schools, that we managed to contain Halesworth within those ten prizes, which amounted, as I have said, to 25% of all the prizes in their age-group.

I have gone into detail about her place in the W. H. Smith Competition because no other context sets the two most striking features of her results – their sheer quantity and their sheer quality – so clearly in an historical as well as a national perspective. And no other context could give such a vivid sense of the educational implications of what she is doing. Her pupils have triumphed as brilliantly in other similar competitions, but their performance in this one will serve to set in the reader's mind the full weight of the question: how does she do it?

Her lucid, fascinating and all-too-brief chapters will help to answer that. But it is worth directing attention, I think, towards what seems to be one of the keys to her success.

Wherever a teacher produces a group of talented young writers, their work always shares certain identifying features. In the work from Halesworth, these family features are of a very significant kind, and provide clues, I believe, to Jill Pirrie's ability to unlock the resource of so many of her pupils.

The range of their work is actually rather wide, from re-creation of Bible stories and mythic fables at one extreme to studies in minutely detailed observation at the other. The characteristic Halesworth imprint appears most clearly in these observation exercises – the five finger exercises of Jill Pirrie's method. It appears partly in a particular style of radiant, detailed (sometimes microscopic) observation, but much more, I think, in a certain overtone which the style carries. This overtone expresses the effort – the constantly-renewed and intensely-focused effort – to be precise and honest in observation and word, and to infuse all perceptions with a personal, firsthand guarantee; as if the whole aim of the exercise were not to shape a small work of art, but simply to practise this effort towards precision and honesty. One result of this is a little odd: even though the piece of writing turns out to be a beautiful little poem or paragraph, as it very often does, it always has the air of being a by-product of a more serious purpose; the felicities of image, word and music, no matter how remarkable they may be, remain secondary and incidental. But that is not all.

As she describes in her first paragraphs, Jill Pirrie's crucial opening move is to give her pupils the confidence of their own impressions. In a clearly observable way, everything flows from this basic essential. One can see how it enables her young writers to find a vein of firsthand, living truth in anything they touch. It enables them to make anything their own, and to bring anything to life, simply by finding something of their own life in it: their own memory, fantasies, feelings, thoughts, viewpoint, associations. The 'subjectivity' of this approach is disciplined by the overall pursuit of 'objective precision'. In this way, the rich, intimate hoard of the pupil's inner life is given the role of expressive and interpretative means, in the job of coming to terms with the things of the world.

To some degree, all attempts to interpret the outer world must use these 'subjective' points of reference and sources of insight. What is decisive here, in Jill Pirrie's method, is the unique emphasis she places on consciously developing and refining, in her pupils, a facility with this infinite vocabulary of personal and perhaps secret impressions. It is easy to see what the gains are, where a pupil makes the shift, and begins to draw on such secure, personal resources. Meticulous objectivity is opened to psychological depth and to subjective vitality. By nurturing this in her pupils, Jill Pirrie has freed them from the little-ease of descriptive 'objectivity' – where the scope of 'objectivity' is defined by the spiritless pedantry of the inane – and liberated them into the imaginative objectivity which has produced, in its day, Einstein as well as Shakespeare.

Exercises in this new 'vocabulary' must in the end have a pervasive effect on the whole mentality and well-being, something of which shows, perhaps, in the curiously mature flexibility of viewpoint which the Halesworth children share. Research has revealed conclusively how an awakening of – even a dogged and laborious attempt to awaken – the aesthetic, creative faculties enhances, measurably, all the more 'scientifically inclined' functions of the brain. Controlled, as it is in Jill Pirrie's class, by her governing concern – her classic, Confucian concern – with the primacy of the bond between word and thing, this sort of training begins to resemble a spiritual discipline. At this point, while attaining its immediate, practical ends a great deal more fruitfully, the teaching of written English has become something much bigger than normal classwork.

Simple priorities, then, enable Jill Pirrie not only to teach, but also to transform her pupils. She not only supplies them with a superior kit of language techniques (and an understanding of literature), she lifts them into a special state of mind where new resources become accessible, and where their brains perform, quite naturally feats of interconnection and perception which were previously unthinkable for them. And all the evidence of their work suggests that this state of mind has become the norm in her classes. It is a new order of 'ordinary', from which these admirable poems and paragraphs flow as a natural by-product: nothing else can explain their extraordinary abundance and quality. Even the most backward pupils, as Jill Pirrie describes, are able to take part in this new freedom of 'ordinariness' which is surely a confirmation of how soundly based and human her principles are.

Obviously, there is still a great deal more to it. And no doubt, since what teachers teach is chiefly themselves as human beings, the final clue to Halesworth's mystery lies well behind these pages, hidden within Jill Pirrie herself. If she is the tuning fork, to which all her pupils become so attuned, there remain several questions – unanswerable ones, I imagine – to be asked about the components of the tone she has established. Nevertheless, these pages, and the poems by her pupils which illustrate them, supply many suggestive clues to that clue.

Ted Hughes, 1987

# 1 Introduction

This book is, in essence, a collection of children's writings. As many of the pieces have won awards in national competitions, I have been asked repeatedly why and how these children achieve their standard. The workings of the imagination are always mysterious and not always linked with the kind of intelligence which will win academic success. Consequently, it is very difficult to explain 'successful' imaginative writing. However, I have attempted here to explore the basic philosophy of my teaching and, in particular, some of the strategies which have produced these poems.

It has become a truism that children must write from their personal firsthand experience. While it is easy to accept that personal experience is the basis of all good imaginative writing, it is not easy to resolve the classroom problems which arise from this premiss. Children crave excitement. Their own worlds seem pale and humdrum beside the worlds which they feel capable of inventing. Their instinct is to reject their own world and to 'make up' stories and poems which, unhappily, are so often no more than banal, unconvincing flights of fancy. Paradoxically, the teacher must set boundaries, impose constraints, in order to set

free. When we ask children to imagine, we are, above all, asking them to remember with a special intensity. Only then do we establish an authentic starting point for their writing. And so, two clear problems emerge:

*1.* How do we transform the limited, 'ordinary' experience of the child so that he turns to it as a source of interest and excitement, willing to relive it in a state of total involvement?

*2.* How, having achieved this involvement, do we help the child towards a position of detachment from which he can apply his craft as conscious artist, subject to the rigour of his discipline? I have found that these problems can be resolved only through a literature-based curriculum. There must be excitement. When we read, excitement comes through a vital moment of connection with the text. This is a moment when we recognise something we have noticed ourselves but never before truly realised, something which has been brought to our attention by the seeing eye of the writer. At one of these moments of recognition or identification comes a sense of surprised discovery. Suddenly our own experience attains new value. It is exciting, worth taking seriously. There is an episode in Barry Hines' *Kes* which unfailingly provides a class with a literary experience of this kind. The scene is a classroom in a run down urban school. The children are disadvantaged, inarticulate. One boy, Anderson, called upon to address the class, stands miserably silent. He can think of nothing worth talking about. The teacher urges

'just something you've remembered'.

Memory stirs. But Anderson is embarrassed. His own experience is too limited, too trivial to put into words. Shamefaced, he replies:

'There's summat. it's nowt though.'

The teacher's reply is crucial:

'It must be if you remember it.'

And so Anderson is released. No longer inarticulate, he tells his sensuous, exciting story of two small boys filling their wellies with tadpoles. One of those boys, Anderson himself, puts on the tadpole filled wellies. Taddies squash between his toes, spurt up his legs, and, of course, our own children cannot fail to make the connection. Like the class in the novel, they are

'up to the knees in tadpoles'.

Most importantly, through a literary experience, their own ordinary lives have been heightened. For a moment, they turn to the trivia of their own world with a sense of discovery; they make a first, tentative step on the journey to self-acceptance. In the classroom, these fleeting moments cannot be harnessed at will, but we can be sure that our children's writing will testify to their reality. The poems which follow, for example, were written by children whose 'nowt' had suddenly become 'summat'.

Feeding Time

Two ponies await me
As I walk out in snow to the rims of my boots.
The snow melts
And milk runs down a bottle
Where a bluetit pecked at a silver lid.
My ponies whinny, an echo in a dark cave,
As I carry two sections of hay,
Hazel and yellow,
Its summer green mellowed by the sun.

The grey pony – mud right up to her hocks,
Her muzzle rough with the coarse hairs,
Eyes dark blue with a sense of understanding,
Winter coat furry,
Not white against the snow
But shaded like a tree.
And her ears, dainty dolls, pricked to attention.
The other pony, smaller but wary,
His coat a patchwork of mud

On end to attack the winter winds.
Ears, one forward, the other, back,
Curved in like a bent nail.

I put the hay down and watch them eat.
They munch, their teeth worn, yellow,
And I walk away, filling my page,
Back through the snow to my house.

*Ruth Hooton 10 years*


The Tree Climb

The plum tree, rough and rotten,
Crumbles under my numb hands.
The branches are old
And as I climb, they shudder beneath me,
The blossom streaming off in angry chains, pink and fluffy.
Close up, I see the grooves and wrinkles in the trunk;
I smell the rough pattern of the red leaves
And can almost taste the rusty bark.
In the centre of the tree
I am in my own rainbow world,
Cut off from traffic, people, noise,
Everything.
Everything, except the blossom and the smell of
    the scarlet bark.
I climb down and the tree is still
And almost scary.
The garden is deserted – beneath the fluffing branches,
And the falling blossom.

*Matthew Shepherd 10 years*


Ploughing

The tractor roars, pulls away
at the three-furrow plough.

Sparks shatter, twisted metal
strikes a flint
hidden under the earth.

The ash, as it hits the red hot
robin's breast, floats away
into the dark to lighten sunset.

The engine eases.
Shadows, my thumb as long as a pencil,
as the sun dies.

Silence covers
the countryside.

*Trevor Guyton 12 years*


Fossil

I look at my fossil collection
Slowly I drift to far off caves,
The walls charred and rough,
Charcoal pictures on rock, faded by the ages,
The emptiness hollow and flat.
A crack in the wall splits the emptiness in two,
Like a tree split by lightning.
The mouth of the cave:
A burnt out fire, dead ashes blowing in the wind,
Crumbling like old paper.
Black, cracked wood lies forgotten on the floor,
Turned to charcoal.
The ages have polished flints;
Here time stands still,
Grey, like the rocks,
Grey, like my fossil.

*Peter Watts 10 years*


The Pond

Once, there was a pond in our garden,
With carp, their rainbow armour plating
Making rainbow men dance
In the shimmering water.
Now, the carp lies dead,
Its armour dull, as if unpolished.
Once, there was a pond in our garden,
With coots, their little ones beaky pom-pom balls
Bobbing along after their mother's ripples.
Now, the coot has flown,
Leaving her young lifeless in the ramshackle nest.
Once, there was a pond in our garden
With water lilies tethered on green strings,
Blooming upturned parachute flowers.
Now, their tethers frayed,
They lie on the dry, crazy-paving reed bed.

Once, there was a pond in our garden,
With . . .
What?

*Jude Fitzgerald 11 years*

Memory is, of course, only the first stage (albeit a crucial one) in the imaginative process. The child poet remembers first, then selects and patterns. It is in these subsequent stages, the moment of conscious expression, that he detaches himself from his experience. Herein lies another intriguing paradox: these young poets must be childlike, artless, and yet, at the same time, artful. It is the teacher's dilemma to resolve this paradox. Again my own solution lies within literature: in this case Ted Hughes' poem 'Thought-Fox', followed by a reading of the poet's own explanation of the poetic process in *Poetry In the Making*. In his explanation, Ted Hughes shares with the children the way in which the 'Thought-Fox' came to be written. He lets them into a secret (and secrets are always exciting!) As fellow writers, they listen and begin to grasp this underlying paradox of the poet's task, between the intensity of his involvement in his subject and the detachment he needs to subject this material to the poetic process. Within the resolution of this paradox lies the tension from which poetry is made. Hughes' statement:

'It is a fox and a spirit. It is a real fox.'

shows us that a fox in a poem is at once a particular fox, and one which contains something of all foxes everywhere. The children's attempts to write their own 'Thought-Creature' poems must also be based upon close and accurate observation of one particular creature. But they must also aspire towards universality; they must represent spirit as well as substance. I have found 12 to 13 year olds quite capable of appreciating the complexity of their task and yet excited, rather than daunted by it. The less able grasp it at an intuitive level and often, surprisingly, write with a particular strength and clarity.

### The Dog

The dog lies in the mist of my mind,
And then he steps forward out of the mist
And into my memory.

The dog steps cautiously,
Scared of something but not knowing what;
He follows the passage round a corner,
And in the distance light appears.

He tries to run from it but the light
Drags him towards the opening ahead,
Then he shoots into an arena packed with words.

The dog felt drunk, his black tail
Swishing excitedly and his stumpy legs
Were no longer supporting him.

Then the dog felt himself changing.
He looked down and he himself
Had turned into a word,
Ready to be chosen and put on the
Poet's paper.

*Andrew Holmes  13 years*


The Thought-Bird

My mind receives the falling snow,
Which is whiter than life,
Beautiful and delicate.
I think of the soft song of the white bird as it sits on the
    chimney pot watching its feathers fall.
The carol singers sing and the street lights blend
With the bird and the snow.
The wind whispers, 'Not a sound, not a sound'.
The carol singers fade away
Into this white and beautiful night.
My mind is still in harmony with this bleak bird
Which has fluttered from thoughts into my words.

*Gregory Block  13 years*


And so the children begin to realise that the raw material of poetry exists trapped within their minds. In so far as all children have memories, all children are embryo poets. Occasionally a child may be word deaf in the same way as another is tone deaf. This is rare, however.

John Gordon, one of our leading writers for children, says in his essay in *The Thorny Paradise*, 'On Firm Ground',

> 'The starting point must be a place which already exists, we cannot free ourselves from what we know, and Mars is still landscaped on earth. A rigidity is necessary; imagination must be anchored . . .'

As teachers we must accept and teach the terms of this rigidity. Only then can we set children free to achieve some small part of their potential.

## 2 Process

Much of the teacher's task lies in guiding children through the process of writing, while at the same time preserving the freshness and spontaneity which must be the hallmark of their work. I have found the following exercises teach structure and, at the same time, respect the integrity of the writer's ideas.

To begin with, a reading of Jacques Prévert's 'To Paint the Portrait of a Bird'. The work which follows has something in common with Sandy Brownjohn's 'The Making of . . .' exercise described in *What Rhymes With Secret?* In many ways the painting of a picture is like the writing of a poem and a reading of 'To Paint the Portrait of a Bird' directs attention to the way in which we handle words. Clearly, the Noun/Name is the strongest part of speech. The children see that, as poets, they are, above all, Namers. They learn that each individual has his own identity contained within his uniquely magical first name. Power lies in that first name. As poets we must search rigorously for the right Name or the spell won't work.

Secondly, they come to see the Verb as second in importance only to the Noun. Again its effectiveness lies in the precision of its use. As the poet's tool, it must be fine, resilient, appropriate to its task. Similarly, what better way to learn familiarity with these common grammatical terms than within a context of reading and writing poetry. At the same time the children learn the strength of the active, the comparative weakness of the passive. They practise making conscious, delicate decisions. They discover how complex is the poet's task when he tries to write most simply and clearly. This exercise can come as a necessary corrective to the intelligent, 'literary' child whose writing all too easily becomes loose with ill-chosen or redundant adjectives or adverbs. Children must learn to write with economy and discrimination, and to guard jealously the power of their nouns. They must also discover that there are no rules which cannot sometimes be broken to good effect. Always I stress that poetry is written to be spoken, that sound and meaning must harmonise. They must develop an ear sensitive to the music of their words.

Jacques Prévert's poem also teaches something of the seriousness of the artist-poet's work, the depth of his commitment as he waits for the idea:

> 'Sometimes the bird comes quickly
> but he can just as well spend long years
> before deciding
> Don't get discouraged
> wait
> wait years if necessary.'

And . . .

> 'When the bird comes
> if he comes
> observe the most profound silence.'

Ideas, like birds, are elusive and I believe a deep, relaxed silence is necessary if children are to write poetry. The classroom is normally an unsatisfactory environment for writers. The close proximity of so many bodies means endless distraction, but these children at least deserve silence.

Then there is the insistence that we judge our work by the highest standards:

> 'If the bird doesn't sing
> it's a bad sign
> a sign that the painting is bad
> but if he sings it's a good sign
> a sign that you can sign . . .'

And so the children write their own 'To Paint a . . .' poems. Again they try to balance an intense memory of their subject with the conscious detachment which chooses only the best materials and wields the truest tools. They do not copy or parody. Rather, Jacques Prévert has provided them with a framework for their own perceptions and observations. Through receiving his voice, they find their own. I hope that this is at its best the 'creative mimesis' which Peter Abbs argues for so strongly in *English Within the Arts*. At times the children's writing is clear, strong and simple. When it is, they have reconciled the subjective and objective aspects of their craft.

### Transformation

I watch as a ship sails serenely by.
And using my mind as a pencil,
My eyes as paints,
I sketch a warship from the waves.
And my pencil
Turns the blue-grey sea
Into blue-grey steel.
As a stupendous wave whirls up,
A transformation is made
From wave to ship's chimney,
From foam to smoke,

Vanishing into space.
My eyes turn to land,
The barren, brown land.
It distorts into another warship,
Not modern now, wooden.
From Hermes to Mary Rose.
As a lifeguard's flag comes into sight,
She has a pinnace now – and life.

*Alison Enticknap 12 years*

## To Paint a Garden

First, mix a muddy brown
And pour it onto the paper.
Swish and swirl it around
With your brush.
Then paint in:
The patter of insects' feet,
The smell of compost,
The hardness of stones.
Then paint a fence
Surrounding the garden;
Draw grey metal strips
Criss-crossing each other;
Then add the coldness and hardness.
In one corner
Paint a solitary spade
Leaning on the fence.
Paint a rough wooden handle,
Worn with use,
And a blunt edge for the blade.
Now paint in:
Vegetables, fruit, flowers –
All different colours and shapes.
Add the smell of insects,
And there is a garden.
Then paint in a cloud,
A cloud full of water.
And make it rain –
To leave your garden
Fresh and clean.

*Michelle Brooham 13 years*

I include the following poem written as a result of the Sandy Brownjohn exercise 'The Making Of . . .'; firstly, because it has much in common with the foregoing poems, and secondly, because it demonstrates a delightful sense of fun. Poetry writing of all kinds demands complete commitment; this does not preclude enjoyment. The two are interdependent.

## The Making of a Hornet

For the body,
Take a piece from dad's best rugby shirt,
Shrink it,
In a wash that is far too hot,
Dry it,
In mother's new tumble-dryer,
Crimp it
In your oldest sister's crimper.

For the wing,
Make up the recipe for glass.
Bake
In hot oven till soft;
Roll out with gran's best rolling pin;
Cut
In two and stick firmly to body.

For the legs
Untangle eight of the hairs from grandad's beard.
Intertwine
Two together so you have four pairs.

For the brain
Unhook Aunt Maeve's best duffle coat.
Cut out
The British Home Stores ticket inside.
Feed it with knowledge for five days,
Then let it breathe in a dark cupboard.

For the buzz
Take the first sound your telly makes
When you switch it on.
Then nourish it on other buzzes.
Next,
Embroider this buzz into the brain.

Then roll up into a ball,
Flutter his wings
And let him call.

*Rachel Harrison 12 years*

Following this exercise comes a reading of extracts from writers' notebooks. Access to writers' notebooks gives the children a sense of privilege. They feel initiated into the secret world of the writer's mind and again there is that essential ingredient of excitement. Gerard Manley Hopkins' detailed observations of water, the way it behaves, the manner in which a wave breaks, are read alongside artist Leonardo da Vinci's detailed recordings of trees, water, creatures reproduced in *Penguin English Stage One: I Took My Mind A Walk*. The details of the observations are impressive. The fact that writers may keep notebooks in much the same way that artists may keep sketchpads has wide implications for the children. Most especially they begin to appreciate the need for constant re-drafting. And so, they attempt a simple prose account of a process they have observed or attempted themselves. It may be a craftsman at work, the way in which a fire burns, anything which requires of them a detailed analysis of the process and then a careful drafting and re-drafting until a piece of clear, accurate prose emerges:

Unblocking a Drain in Winter

The water started to gurgle above the drain grate. The day was cold and the water had a thin layer of ice on the top of it. I took a good hold of the glove. It was frozen solid. I held the glove tight and smashed it on a wall, over and over. A shower of jagged ice fragments fell to the ground and broke into a thousand pieces of glittering beads.

The glove was big and had about half an inch spare on each finger. The water inside the glove froze on my hand like setting jelly. I walked over to the drain and bent over and clamped my fingers under the grate. It reminded me of a spider's web. The coldness soon penetrated the rubber glove and I hadn't even put my hands in the water. Cramp soon set in so I had to stop. I sat down with my hands in the air watching my fingers straighten out until they could not move. I sat in a certain amount of pain waiting for my fingers to right themselves.

For the second time I tried to unblock the drain, I put my hand in the water. I reached down to find the bottom but the water started to seep over the top of the glove. It ran down the inside and started to fill up each of the fingers. As the water rose in each finger the cramp began. I stood up and flung the glove, water spraying on the ground. I sat on the ground and started huffing and puffing on my hands to keep them warm. Bother the glove! I just stuck my hand in and cleared it. I felt the bottom and scooped a handful of mud and leaves out. My hand was like a mechanical digger. I brought out five loads of mess. A job well done.

*Ian Self 12 years*

**Naming Through the Senses**

The 1960s made central the child and his experience, particularly the way in which we all explore the world through our senses. There is no doubt that this preoccupation led to certain excesses. Sometimes the pouring out of sensuous detail was unselective and unstructured. Nevertheless, there was excitement in the genuine attempt to enable children to write honestly. Today we must remember that the senses are not only the means by which we explore the world and know that we are alive; they are also the means by which we remember. Past events are recalled by a fleeting, evocative smell, an associated sound; we see with our 'mind's eye' when we recall. Hence, when we ask children to imagine, the sharpness of their perceptions derives directly from sense impressions. While the 1960s emphasised sensuous experience, previous decades required that great writers be absorbed and imitated. Today, I suggest, the way forward lies in a synthesis of these attitudes. By reading a wide range of fiction and poetry, children absorb the symbols of our culture; by listening to the cadences and rhythms of others, they learn structure and find their own voice. The following exercise took place within a context of reading and speaking a wide range of poetry.

First – a matter of drafting, note making: *Remember a creature you have watched closely and write five observations, each one relating to one of your five senses.*

*Magpie*

| | |
|---|---|
| *1. Touch:* | The smooth black feathers with a rough edge, the hard plastic beak and twig-tree legs. |
| *2. Sight:* | The graceful flight as it snaps a fly in mid-air and the clumsy, drunken walk, the sea-green blaze on its back. |
| *3. Hearing:* | The rasping morning cry and the scrape of claws on metal. |
| *4/5. Taste/Smell:* | The stench of magpie droppings that finds its way into your nose so you can taste it in your throat. |

*Joanne Leverett 12 years*

This is, of course, an artificial exercise. Our senses are interdependent and cannot be classified in this way. Nevertheless, it harnessed an act of intense memory to the necessary self-consciousness of the poet. Later the poem emerged from these notes through an act of deliberate craftsmanship:

My Magpie

She was a thing of beauty.
The sea-green blaze on her back
Flashed in the sun
As she gracefully snapped a fly
In mid-air.
Her drunken walk across the lawn to her food bowl
Will live in my memory.
I miss her screech, her rasping morning cry
    outside my window.
She would attack my blowing hair in the wind.

Under the cat's watchful eye,
I would hold out a piece of milk soaked bread.
She would hop, reproachful, nearer –
And – 'Arrgh,' like a sailor.
Often I would stroke her.
Her black beak was as sharp as a cat's grip,
Hard and plastic,
The stench of magpie droppings
Hung in my throat,
Heavy like my tonsils;
But then I lost my black beauty –
The cat's eye became his teeth.

*Joanne Leverett 12 years*

The following poems similarly show deliberate recall of sense impressions crafted into an art form:

Leaving of Swallows

Swallows pinned on an electric wire
Like clothes pegs on a line.
The angry wire bounced in retaliation;
So did the swallows, playfully.
As they carried their white bellies,
They passed baton like messages
To one another.
At the far end sat an old Grandma Swallow,
Or so I thought:
Like an old retired office cleaner,
She stayed head under wing.

They raced and they chased
Through the air like fire.
Brown tinted feathers caught the sun
And glistened like rubies.
It was just like watching ice skaters,
But even better; they didn't need years of practice.
They were already perfect, and
Ready to set off on their long journey.

Through the sky they softly faded,
Fading like soft smudged pencil dots.

*Gail Bloomfield 13 years*

Senses

Taste
The dry, musty leaves
Which tamper with the air.
Lingering smoke,
The taste of ash.

Hear
The clip of the shears
As they prune the hedge.
Listen to the leaves
As they throw a tantrum
In the wind.

Smell
The sweet fragrance
From soft brown apples
Feasted by wasps,
The dusty corn
Thrown from the yellow harvester.

See
The rust colour
Painted through the garden.
See the bee,
Flying,
Weighed down by boots of yellow pollen.

Touch
The leaves
Crumbling with dryness.
Feel the bitter night
In the air
Of my autumn garden.

*Ruth Kingshott 13 years*


Morning Cow

The morning cow stands at the gate.
   Solid as a brick wall, hard and strong,
The wet slime from its mouth
   Like a frozen waterfall.
Then, a strong biting sound
   From a never-ending hollow hole,
Where warm smoke appears.
   Its tail acts like a fly swatter,
   hanging like a plumb line.

Its feet look like solid lumps of metal,
    Shaped like axes ready to cut.
The grass it stands on is jewelled with
    Water like fresh cut coins.
The gate opens,
    And the noise of the hooves
Sends earthquakes to Australia.

*Darren Pearce  11 years*


Pheasant Chick

I scoop desperately to catch a chick,
    but fail.
Then I corner one,
a mirrored image of a puff clock.

I take the fragile scaffolding of bones,
and rest it on my palm,
sticky like Blu-tack.

After a struggle the puff clock uncoils,
and stands on cranefly legs.
The eyes, sunk in the skull, are bright
    and shiny,
like my tiny pearl marbles.
Its beak snaps shut and springs open,
like a mouse trap.

It struggles;
I put it down,
and it screams back to the
    mother brooder.

*Caroline English  12 years*


Dancing Butterflies

Fields burn like rabbits moulting.
The black ash floats
And drifts with the wind.
My hand feels the polluted air
But all it feels are the rare black butterflies tickling.
The dead fields are charcoal black
And the hedge's fringe is singed.
The wind whistles the melody
To which the butterflies dance.

They rise and subside in all directions.
The wind whistles no more.
The butterflies fall and die
And leave a black carpet
For you to tread on.

*Gregory Block  13 years*


Polks the Goat

Polks –
Her ears are sagging wings,
her coarse fur like marram grass;
as she walks, her soufflé udder
pulls downwards, getting heavier;
a pile of aniseed balls trails behind her.

The milk hits the metal pail
with a ring.
It froths like soapy water.
The udder is empty
and hangs, an empty balloon.

She bleats,
an opera singer with a sore throat.
The roughness of her fur makes your hand feel numb.
Her fur covered horns jut out like knuckles on a clenched
fist
ready to hit and butt.
She feeds;
the door is bolted.
We go with the churn.

*Katy Bremner  13 years*

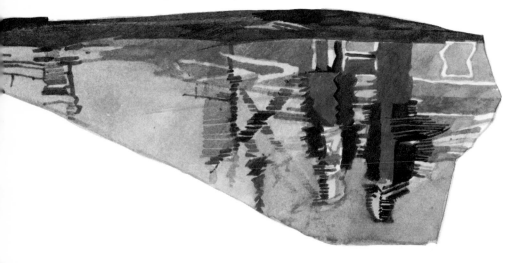

## 3 Ways of Looking

Our children must learn that if their poetry is to work it must surprise. Moreover, they must realise that it is the poet's especial task to reveal the surprising within the ordinary. I have found the following exercise – 'The Magic Image' – a means of discovering the bizarre, the surreal, where we least expect it; in the everyday. This everyday world, as we receive it through our senses, is unstable, fluid and shifting. Constantly, we are the victims of delusion. Our eyes are deceived by tricks of the light, shadows, reflections. Eroded rocks become menacing faces; cracks in the ceiling move and pattern as we stare at them.

We begin the exercise by reading 'Water Picture' by May Swenson. Here the illusion of reflection makes 'magic images' in such a way that we find the extraordinary within the familiar. As usual, we have all seen these images. But we have not realised them. May Swenson, because she is a poet, awakens us to these facets of our past 'ordinary' experiences. Again, this is a moment of identification with the text when that vital connection is made and our own experience realised and externalised. Further, when we look at a reflection as though for the first time we cannot help but write in metaphor. We simply accept the evidence of our eyes in a childlike poetic way. Usually when we look at a reflection in a window our mind censors what we see so that we separate the three layers – the glass, the reflection, the scene outside. It is when we resist this censorship and look with the poet's eye that we enter a bizarre, surreal world in which

> 'The newsreader sits
> Talking in the garden;
> The cats tread on his face.'

> *Thorsten Merriott 12 years*

or in which

> 'My face is a pond.
> The outside fence surrounds
> My nose, a goldfish
> Breathing . . .'

> *Victoria Mawer 12 years*

Following this comes a reading of 'Images' by George Tardios. His opening words:

> 'The world is troubled
> With a lack of looking.'

are the basis of discussion – if only we would look, we would find the magical within the commonplace. Again, we see that the world, as we receive it through our senses, is not stable but subject to change, illogicality. Sometimes our own response to the world connives with the illusion to make a deeper magic:

> 'I see the sky reflected in my teacup.
> I move the cup
> and I tilt the sky.'

> *George Tardios*

Many of the 'Images' poems written as a result of this exercise are a response to the comic: the serious made foolish, the upside-down, the inside-out, the back-to-front. There is, in most of the poems, a delighted recognition of the foolishness of human beings at the mercy of their sensuous experience. Children also discover that in a poem an image may be auditory, olfactory, or tactile, as well as visual. For instance, the subject 'Echoes' may well come within the scope of the 'Magic Image'.

I find that not only does this exercise produce worthwhile writing; it is also, and perhaps more importantly, a key point in the process by which the child learns to make connections, sometimes bizarre, in order to arrive at a greater truth.

Reflection

As the eyes of my mind
Slip across the planes of sand,
The waves retreat from the shore
And the spray returns –
To the watery sky.

The clouds sink above;
My footsteps run to the foam,
Glazed with sunset.

A boat bobs on the sea of clouds
And forests of seaweed appear
On the horizon.

Fish fly
As the winded seagulls dart through spray
Deceiving me.

*Kay Chambers 12 years*

Reflections

Plop,
the bait, the weight and the fishing line
explore the water.
Ripples spread;
they expand,
then swim away.
The water again still.

Like the beach
the pebbles vary in size.
My reflection lies on them,
like a sunbather.

An old tin can for my face,
my fishing line entangled in my hair.

The tree behind me
lies over my body
but I don't feel squashed.
I didn't hear it splash the water.
I am confused.

A bite!
I catch a fish.
It swims right through me.
Untangling the fishing line,
I pull my fish out.
I must have pulled myself out too.
For I look again and I see –
just ripples.

*Ruth Kingshott 12 years*

Reflection in a Window
The misty image of the garden,
Still,
Still with the power of loneliness,
Alive with the horror of darkness.
The light streams out like a tidal wave
Flooding from the car headlights.
The condensation on the window pane regroups,
Rolls downwards,
As the newsreader outside
Announces more rain.
The telegraph pole stands like a soldier,
Proud,
Guarding the garden.
The stars are watching over him,
Like the buttons from the soldier's coat.
But then the light goes out
And the room joins the outside
In darkness
Darker than a hole.

*Karl Andrews 12 years*

Floating Images

Clouded lilies,
golden from the morning sun,
part,
revealing broken windows
filtered with mud
and grime.

A sparrow,
caught in the weeds,
is trapped like a genie
in a bottle.
I stand on my head,
bouncing
on a trampoline sky
as frogs leap
from building to building
flying three metre gaps.
Trees are like bushes
on crutches,
wobbling.
Two footballs appear
heading towards each other
closer, closer . . .
Splop.
They turn into one.
The pool ages.
It grows wrinkles
that move.
Skyscrapers melt away,
bushes die
and frogs disappear
under skinny waters.
The pond is still,
except for a bobbing ball.

*Scott Dougal 12 years*


Water Reflection

Seaweed for hair,
Pebbles for eyes
And two cockles,
One a mouth and
One a nose.
Wide eyed I stare
And the face
Stares back.

A fish swims in
One ear and
Out the other.
It disturbs the water
And a piece of hair

Breaks away and
Floats downstream
Followed by the rest
Of the face . . .

*Rachel Flaxman  12 years*

## Seen Through the Lens

Again, the theme is the 'Magic Image', and the purpose is to make the child
conscious of his looking and aware of the immense difficulty of his task, while at the
same time, releasing the urge to write. When we use a lens, we look with a
deliberation, an intensity. There is a moment of transformation and there are
various facets to the experience: the three stages by which the transformation
occurs. For example, if the lenses belong to binoculars, the stages are:
1. The scene through the naked eye – hazy, indistinct.
2. The act of focusing. The moment of transformation when the sense of sight
   becomes curiously independent of the other senses. We can now see in close up
   but we cannot hear, smell, taste or touch. So we are in the scene but not of it. We
   are detached observers.
3. The binoculars are removed – the scene hazy, indistinct as at first. This poem
   may have a circular shape.
A poem to initiate thinking is 'In the Microscope' by Miroslav Holub. I find also
that good colour photographs of cell structures under a microscope provoke
interest and discussion.

Seen Through a Lens

The rock's grey outline jutted out
Like a filling in an erupting tooth
From a sea of green gum.
A climber hangs from a fishing line rope,
A red spider
Hanging from its thread
Contrasting brightly against
The dull coloured rock.
I lift my binoculars.
Everything has a rainbow edge.
Then,
I see the texture of the rocks
And the wrinkles in a climber's coat and trousers.
I feel the determination
In his expression.
It is as though I can feel the whistle
Of the wind
And the rustle of his anorak.
I put down my binoculars

And once again the rock juts out greyly
And the climber is
The spider, small and vulnerable,
Hanging from its thread.

*Stephen Cook  12 years*


Seen Through the Lens

A motion of clothes,
A stick as thin as a single
Horse's hair.
He sits on a matchbox waiting, soundless.

A circle of perfection,
A magic, magnifying circle.
The sleeve of his jumper, dirty
Where he put his hand in the maggot box.

The pond has mini-waves,
Tench for whales,
Pike for shark.

His rod tip sways,
Sways silently.
His bream is a shark,
His dream is hopeful.

A motion of clothes,
A stick as thin as a single
Horse's hair.
He sits on a matchbox,
        Hopeful.

*Trevor Guyton  12 years*

## 4 What is the Truth?

I have found *What Is The Truth?* by Ted Hughes one of the most exciting and challenging books to be published for children in recent years. Subtitled 'A Farmyard Fable For The Young', it is an anthology of poetry with the poems linked by connecting prose passages continuing the theme of fable. This fable theme gives the poems an underlying meaning which persuades children into considering the nature of their own imaginative writing. Story is, of course, the proper vehicle for such abstractions. Children are able to apprehend the abstract at a very early age when it comes to them in this guise.

The book begins with God's Son being curious; he wants to find out about this earth and, in particular, mankind. He asks his Father to take him on a visit to earth;

'travel broadens the mind.'

God is doubtful:

'Mankind cannot teach you anything. Mankind thinks it knows everything. It knows everything but the Truth.'

The Son persists and, at last, God leads him to a village hillside and proceeds to summon the villagers to ask them questions in an attempt to arrive at the Truth. The farmer comes first. His task is deceptively simple:

'Tell us about one of the creatures on your farm.'

The farmer speaks poetry but finds the 'Truth' of the partridge strangely elusive. One by one the villagers speak poems about the creatures they know so well. Some come tantalisingly close to the 'Truth'. Always, however, the linking prose pieces keep in mind the futility of the poet's search. It is a fruitless search because it is endless. Words are clumsy, slippery. When patterned into metaphor they sometimes almost find Truth.

In this fable, however, God is consistently dissatisfied with the villagers' efforts. Here is the ultimate criterion by which poetry is judged. Sometimes He is pleased because there is so much surprise and delight in images coined so unusually and yet truthfully, of cows:

'And there's a ruined holy city
In a herd of lying down, and chewing cows.'

of farm horses:

'huge plum tight haunches revolving heavily
like mill wheels.'

of swallows:

'Blue splinters of queer metal. . .'

God's dissatisfaction with the poems as a whole is, of course, the supreme dissatisfaction of the poet – however he chooses and patterns his words, the permutations are endless, limited only by our human condition.

Paradoxically, however, the situation is not hopeless. If only we could put the right words in the right order, then we would arrive at the Truth. The *possibility* is always there. In a way these villagers are trying to emulate God's act of creation when He named these creatures and they came into being. The villagers' naming can be an approximation only. And yet again and again Ted Hughes makes us feel that it is indeed possible. We are even made to feel that, given the right words, the flesh and blood creature would appear before our very eyes; such would be the power of its Naming. Intellectually, however, we know such a power is beyond the greatest of poets. In fact, the nearer we come to the Truth, the more we realise our distance from it. And excitement builds. Throughout the book there is the tension of knowing that, in the end, the onus will be on God to answer His Son's question:

> 'But have we heard the Truth?' asked God's Son. He still had no idea what the Truth might be.
> 'No, not the Truth,' said God sadly. 'Not the Truth.'
> 'Then tell us the Truth,' said God's Son. 'What is the Truth?'
> 'The Truth,' said God finally, 'is this. The Truth is that *I* was those worms . . . And the Truth is,' God went on, 'that *I* was that Fox. Just as *I* was that Foal . . . I am each of these things. The Rat. The Fly. And each of these things is Me . . . It is. That is the Truth.'

Unhappily, this is a Truth which we cannot comprehend. The Infinite is beyond our human experience and so we are unable to make the necessary connection. Just as in *Paradise Lost* Satan's accessibility engages our sympathy, while God remains remote and nebulous, so, here, ultimate truth is beyond our grasp. Our preference for Ted Hughes' animal poetry to God's stark

> 'I am each of these things.'

is, however, an affirmation of our human condition rather than a rejection of the Infinite. Again, there is the essential paradox – the only genuine ending to 'What Is The Truth?' is an unsatisfying one. Perhaps most importantly, at the very end, God's Son stays here on Earth. Further, as the dawn rises, there is a doorway:

> 'And the middle of that cloud glowed like the gilded lintel of a doorway that had been rubbed bright.'

It is Man's destiny to aspire to the impossible. And this truth frees the children to make this aspiration their own. They are challenged into a deep commitment to search their memories, find the right words, work within the discipline of the poet's craft in an effort to answer the question *What Is The Truth?* for themselves.

I have found it works well to withhold the actual book from the children until after they have written their own poems. First, the fable can be explained, read to them and some of the poems read aloud. The classroom then becomes the hillside and each child, a villager summoned by God to speak poetry about a creature of the village. That essential ingredient of excitement lies not only in the challenge of the writing but in the eagerness with which, having written their poems, the children search through the book for Ted Hughes' attempt at the Truth of their chosen creature. With the audacity of the young, for a moment, they treat the great poet simply as a fellow writer, like them constrained by his human condition in his search for the Truth. Certainly, this exercise teaches that we succeed as poets only when we know we cannot ultimately do so. This is the paradox which must never be resolved because it provides the tension from which the poet's excitement derives. It is the essential flaw. When children discover it, they develop a deep commitment.

*What Is The Truth?* also helps the teacher in his attitude to assessment of the children's poems. Some teachers feel that they should not judge a child's poem.

They feel they must, at all costs, accept. They feel, moreover, that as a child's poem is an honest attempt to say what he means; if it is criticised, it is debased. I believe that it is possible to respect the integrity of a poem and, at the same time, to criticise positively. The overriding aim, however, is that the children themselves should judge their own poems by the highest criteria. Through a book like *What Is The Truth?* they begin to learn for themselves the supreme dissatisfaction of the poet. Through the story they identify with the villagers and see that, beside ultimate Truth, their efforts are stumbling approximations. They have begun to absorb and understand the criteria they must apply to their own work if they are to write well.

The following poems, I feel, at least contain surprises which aspire towards that universality which comprises something of all starlings, pigs, moles, catfish, Boxer Dogs, rabbits, badgers, fish everywhere. They are brave attempts at the Truth. It is no accident that all these poems have won awards in the W. H. Smith Young Writers' Competition. Such is the magic of *What Is The Truth?* in an ordinary classroom.

The Starling's Truth

Like clouds of anger,
A congregation
Of quick to learn fat-snatchers.
But starlings have to eat.

They darken sunny days,
Swirling in the currents.
Like old sultanas.

Freckled and ragged,
They are complex and confident;
They're Gestapo officers,
Rulers of suburbia.

Terrorising.
Hedge sparrows hastily
Tiptoing from the white and silent world
Of the bird table.

There is no sympathy
In the life of
A starling.

*Andrew Farrow 12 years*

Pigs

A pig, its body like a lump of dough,
Dropped in the mud and squeezed from all its moisture.
Its legs, four pink crayons worn to stubs.

A cork is its nose,
Skewer holes for nostrils,
Clogged with mud and sweat.
It moves along through the muck,
Its hooves dragging, its stomach wobbling,
Like a lazy belly dance.
Its tail a spring, pulled until almost straight.
Dried mud cracks from it as it moves,
Uncovering the pink skin
And small hairs which hold onto muck.
Saliva drips from corners of the mouth
And trickles down its chin,
Leaving a small river of cleanness.

*Lucy Gardner  12 years*


The Badger

A badger is a great, dark bulldozer
Of the wood's undergrowth.
But when in the open
And near man
Is a timid,
Quick moving creature,
Sometimes lifting
Its blunt, wet nose
To take a sniff
For danger.

The vehicle moves
In lumbering jolts,
Snouting and snorting
Inquisitively,
Searching for that
Tasty worm.
A badger is a great, dark bulldozer.

*Jamie MacDonald  12 years*


A Fish

Fish skin like flaky paint
On a gutter.

Its eyes like two wet
Match stains, floating fins,
Shreds of thin ice.

Long black seaweed
Leaves sway on the end
Of its body like a tail.

Its gills, cuttings off finger nails,
Pushes into the
Fish's punctured flesh.

A fish has a spine
Like a bendy wire
For a body a bullet of air
A fish is a fish!

*Gail Bloomfield 13 years*


Four Rabbit Kittens Stare

There four kittens stare,
Cradled over a brick, eight paws settled on a stone.
Four monks kneeling at an altar.

Praying for a careless hand or a forgetful mind.

My hand delves into a sack,
Bringing up corn.
My fist clenched, knuckles tightened, white and rounded
Like a heavy cloud.

Sprinkling the corn into the brick,
It is caught in the rabbit's fur.
Some rain captured.

A rabbit is a beach.
In summer its tidal fur ebbs away.
In winter it gathers round ruffled neck
And splashes surf over chin and under belly.

One whitewashed pebble tossed onto an oil darkened
    beach of fur.
Whiskers are fisherman's tangled line.
Two ears, pricked, sharp, attentive, traced with
    vein like seaweed.

No-one will ever tame a rabbit.

*Stephen Goodwin 13 years*

## The Truth of a Rabbit

Hop, skip and jump,
play and fun
is the rabbit's ambition,
In midair a flick
of its hind legs.
A twirl and
a thrust of dust
and it is off.

An intruder,
a cat or
a rat.
Thud,
frozen still.
Stunned,
as if a ticking
clockwork
that has suddenly stopped.

Its ears a hollow
tree trunk
A river of
transparent veins,
a collar of
rumpled fur.
Its mustard nose
twitching rhythmically
as if listening to music.

Its cheeks covered
in black dots,
from which protrude
long whiskers,
the finest of feelers.
Its front teeth
are of cardboard cutouts.

A black shadow
of nerves and fear,
all but one paw
of white melted wax.
Almost . . .
the truth
of the rabbit?

*Malcolm Goodwin  13 years*

Mole

The mole is a mobile home for worms.
A poor half-sighted labourer
For whom to live is to eat.
His life is subterranean,
A timid animal of the underworld.

He has
Spades for feet,
A drill for a nose,
Two sharp flints for teeth
And a piece of tarred rope for a tail.

The mole is a black velvet purse,
Holding, not money,
But worms.
He is a secret creature,
Who sees no-one
And whom no-one sees.

*Joseph Frost 13 years*

The Silver Catfish

The silver catfish,
Gliding through the melted glass water.
His body,
A rough skeleton,
Covered in a shrimp-like flesh
And gone over with a million miniature fifty pence pieces,
Overlapping like feathers on a bird.
His whiskers reach out and forward,
Like bent needles,
Not quite pulled completely through the material.
Eyes,
Like patterned ping pong balls
That have been pushed through a hole that is too small
And stuck halfway.

He swims,
Dizzily,
Round and round the tank,
His body curving,
Like thread doing running stitch.
Weaving in and out.
A black stripe along his side,
As if a paint brush had been drawn along,
Fading and fading,

As the paint runs out,
Until it finally blends in with his silver scales.

I drop in the fish food –
Flakes,
Like the first crispy topping of pastry
On an apple pie.
He races to the middle;
The water rushes past
His streamline body.
Then, with a flick of his tail,
He shoots up.
His mouth grabs forward
And the food is gone.
Then back he goes
To swim,
Dizzily,
Round the tank.

*Lara Mair 10 years*

A Boxer Dog

A Boxer Dog,
With his pushed in face,
Smells the path
Like a bulldozer.
The dinner on his nose
Stuck like plasticine,
All dry and cracked,
Land without water.
And his teeth
Ground down
Like pegs of wood
Stained yellow.
His tail too,
A stub,
A stub of bone and flesh
Swung from side to side like clockwork,
With difficulty,
As though in need of oiling.
Then he stopped
And his head looked up,
His sad eyes too.
As if to say,
'This is the truth about me.'

*Sally Clifton 11 years*

## 5 Writing for Christmas

In Vol. 3 Issue 1 of *Suffolk Education News* Fred Sedgwick writes:

> '. . . can we have some work . . . that accepts the reality of the Bethlehem event as it probably was? This means a bit of squalor, some cold, a feeling of being left out, and poor, of being a sort of refugee. Heaven knows there is plenty of scope in the world of today for the raw material such work needs . . .
>
> Christmas should bring out the best. And schools look gross arranged like Selfridge shop windows with music arranged by Mantovani, and the poetry supplied by courtesy of Patience Strong.'

Yes, the Christmas story is a tough story and must not be debased in our schools. But because it is a tough story it is a perfect subject for poetry, the toughest language of all. Such is the influence of our consumer society with its accompanying stereotypes and clichés, that it was many years before I dared trust children with the Christmas story as a subject for their writing. Of course, my apprehensions were ill-founded. Children are realists. They are able to slough off the glitter and tinsel and write with an impact and relevance which gives the old story a new universality. If this is to happen, however, there must be direction in the form of constraints imposed by the teacher. Only within those essential constraints will freedom of expression be realised.

A sense of purpose is also vital. In the case of the Christmas poetry which follows, the purpose lay within a sense of audience. This poetry was written for Halesworth's annual concerts of Christmas words and music. For many years I had prepared speakers. Children learned the Christmas poetry of Leonard Clark, Charles Causley, Ted Hughes and many others. They learned the pleasure to be found in entertaining others through performance, and, further, it was a means by which they learned by heart readily and willingly.

I was unwilling to believe that children could write their own Christmas poetry without lapsing into cliché. I was afraid to risk the freshness of their vision. As an adult, above all, I feared sentimentality. Children try to respond appropriately. Would these children of a consumer society produce 'appropriately' stereotyped images of robins in the snow, Bambis sliding on ice? On the other hand, there was the tantalising possibility that they just might express their own vital apprehensions of a story as old as Time and as new as the present moment. They might succeed in telling the toughest story of all in the toughest language of all. Of course, as we saw in *What Is The Truth?* this kind of success is an impossible hope. But within the aspiration to succeed is the energy which will produce exciting poetry. I believe that the various themes which follow, at least, enable these children to write with a freedom and freshness of expression which, at last, I had dared to hope for.

### 'The Visitors'

Clive Sansom's poem 'The Innkeeper's Wife' describes the stable in concrete, everyday images. Many years after the Birth, the innkeeper's widow takes a carpenter into the stable to do repairs and finds her memory stirred.

> 'She rested on the straw, and on her arm
> A child was lying. None of your creased faced brats
> Squalling their lungs out. Just lying there
> As calm as a new-dropped calf.'

Because the visitor is a carpenter, much of the imagery has to do with wood.

> 'Too many memories lurk
> Like worms in this old wood. That piece you're holding –
> That patch of grain with the giant's thumbprint –
> I stared at it a full hour when he died:
> Its grooves are down my mind.'

This language is immediate, the rhythm prose-like, catching the cadences of everyday speech. And these country children were able to make connections. Many muck out stables daily; some have their own horses. Reality began to impinge on tradition. But still a fresh direction was needed. And so, like the carpenter, they came to the stable as visitors, within a particular rôle. Within that rôle, they saw the stable through their own needs, preoccupations, interests, prejudices even. Rôles chosen were both modern and Biblical: artist, scientist, stable boy, soldier, shepherd. The imagery of the familiar stable would be adapted and appropriate to the rôle chosen. Each character would see what he needed to see and what he wanted to see. One child, for example, chose to visit the stable as an artist. For a moment, our own Art room at Halesworth Middle School fused with an event which took place two thousand years ago to produce this poem.


The Christmas Scene Through the Eyes
of an Artist

In through the wind battered door,
a tiny blob of pink oil
Lay in the arms of a woman,
her hair,
like one of my roughest,
thickest brushes.
And her face,
like a canvas scrubbed clean.

The woman lay on blotting paper straw,
soaking up the blood.
A stroke of brown water-colour
held up the roof,
and warped pallet knives,
worn with age,
made a manger.

The oxen; wet nostrils like my mixing trays –
at the end of the day,

their hooves oiled like dry varnish
on a new picture frame,
and the rough,
tired texture of the donkey's hair,
like old pictures from a 1960s' gallery,
gathering dust.

*Kay Chambers 12 years*


Another child found that only when he came as a child was he able to see the Baby. Perhaps already this 12 year old is aware that 'shades of the prison house' are dimming his vision.


The Visitors

A scientist looked through the stable door
And saw millions of molecules,
Swarming like locusts.
He saw chemicals and plant matter
Mixing to form a manger.
He saw blood cells and tissues
Arranged to form mindless beasts:
A horse, an ox, and a cow.

Next came the farmer, pompous and fat,
Peering down at the horse's hooves,
Making sure they were picked and oiled.
Then he checked the straw.
'It hasn't been changed!' he cried.
And stamped off.

Then came the child,
The little stable boy.
Simplicity and fun were all he sought.
Not chemicals and molecules,
Or hooves and straw.
The stable boy – he saw the baby.

*Gary Fenwick 12 years*


A slight variation on this theme is to remember that the Christmas story is not only timeless, it is also universal. Again, to shift time and place may give a new direction and inspire a fresh vision. It is most important, however, to preserve the integrity of the original story. The places chosen for re-enactment must have to do with the poor, the dispossessed, the disadvantaged, the refugee. Above all, at the centre, God is made Man, and even within our secular society the symbolism attached to this idea has a common currency. The following poem takes its imagery from a gipsy encampment.

### Christmas Song of the Crystal Ball

Jangling jewellery flashes
Before my eyes,
Entrances my mind
As the vision clears.

Focus the fire on a symbol of poverty.
Now rats have a branded cross on their backs.
The transformation: Sheep into Serpents, Dogs into Dragons.

Emerge as Romany folk,
Not wanted, self sufficient.
Go camp on no-man's land.

The image, not clear now,
Intersecting.
Cross silver on my palm.
Tyranny to tyranny,
Riches to rags.

And likewise a journey,
On the run. Re-enacting
Soldiers stalk accurately.
Herod's men.
Until, at last, free from bloodshed
The ball is hazy.
The vision is gone.

*Andrew Farrow 12 years*

## The Morning After

Down the ages there have been many variations on the story of the Angels appearing to the Shepherds and the Shepherds' visit to the stable. The 'Morning After' theme explores what happened to them the following morning. Did they return to their hillside overnight, buoyed up by what they had seen? In the cold light of the next morning, what remained? What were their perceptions and feelings as they awoke on the hillside? Did weather and environment reflect those feelings? The following poem, direct and simple, attempts to answer these questions.

The Morning After

I woke to the sight of the ashes,
The half burnt logs, sprawled across the grass
Like half bitten bread.

The glimmer of the sun
Made the coat of the sheep
Silver with dew.

Then I remembered.
The night before,
The baby in the manger,
The horses breathing out liquid nitrogen,
The cow compacting the straw.
And the Baby – not a sound.

Was I there?
Was there a baby?
Was there a horse and a cow?

*Darren Cubbage 12 years*


## The Impossible Christmas

This is another theme which has produced some worthwhile writing. Two lines
from John May's 'Six Things For Christmas' prompted the idea:
> 'I wish to be given beautiful things this Christmas,
> Beautiful but impossible.'

Following the tradition of the Wise Men, Christmas is, above all, a time for gifts.
Again, materialism blunts the keenness of our perceptions. Supposing we could
capture special memories and gift-wrap them. What then would we choose to give
or receive at Christmas? A concept like this must be expressed within a concrete
image if it is to be made accessible. In this way, the children apprehended again
the basic tenet of all their poetry writing: the seat of the imagination is the
memory. And so they made Christmas gift lists. But, this time, 'impossible'
requests: moments, places, people so dear to them that they occupied a special
place in the memory. Having made the list, then, with the conscious detachment of
the poet, they crafted and shaped that list into a poem.

Impossible Gifts

A priceless picture of Christmas,
Framed with a golden summer.
Snow painted like a pink cloud of warm candyfloss,
Bringing with it impossible gifts:
The comfortable feeling of safety,
Warm in our homes
While the rain beats down on a window.

My grandad whom I never saw –
With a face of kind imaginary wrinkles,
Images from treasured photos.
A life to live for the moment
But the knowledge of what lies beyond death,
The last dark secret.
And a box in which to keep my impossible gifts
And a key tied into my head
That only my memory can turn.

*Sally Clifton  12 years*

A variation on the same idea is 'The Impossible Tree'. Here, the usual decorations are dispensed with and the tree is trimmed with images of happiness. Again, the choice is entirely personal, concrete, and derived from memory. Strangely, although working completely independently, the child who wrote the following poem also includes a grandfather whom she had never known. In fact, grandparents appeared in many of the poems – perhaps an intuitive recognition of the importance of our roots in the search for identity.

The Impossible Tree

My tree,
Strewn with simple shapes.
A snowflake,
Melted edges like sucked toffee;
A memory of my first winter,
The trembling spider's web tinsel
Glittering with dew drops.

A shell echoes
The wispy call of the sea,
As I remember
That beach,
The waves breaking on the stony shore.
A cowbell,

Tinkling familiarly as Duppy
Saunters from my mind.
The tinsel
Twists and turns, a web of trouble
Among joy.
And a single puff of smoke,
Lingering on dusty brown photographs
Of my great grandad,
Long gone
Whom I never saw.
And to crown my tree,
The Star of
Bethlehem,
An image in the night sky.

*Rachel Gardam  13 years*


## Winter Poetry

There is always some room for seasonal 'winter' poetry within a Christmas
anthology where the emphasis is on the particular, the specific, the surprising
image derived from the uniqueness of all personal experience. I have found
Charles Tomlinson's 'Winter Piece' a useful starting point because it is so closely
observed. It supplies those vital moments of recognition and identification in
images like:

'Gates snap like gunshot
as you handle them . . .
Ruts with iron flanges track
through a hard decay.'

Ted Hughes has written in *Poetry in the Making*:

'I doubt if much would come of just "snow" as a subject. But there
are an infinite number of categories within the general concept
"snow", and it is the teacher's job to help the pupil narrow the idea
down to a vivid memory or fantasy.'

So often, the teacher's rôle must be that of a narrower down, rather than an opener
up. Paradoxically, when the possibilities are narrowed down, they open up in
remarkable ways. Always, imagination must be anchored in reality. That is where
the excitement lies.


Winter Scene

I surveyed the scene,
My nose flattened
On the window.

My breath steamed the glass
And as I wiped it,
Bony icicles, clinging to the gutter,
Formed a portcullis
Against the fortress of frost.

Its courtyards were flanked with snow
Piped onto the frosty ground
Like smooth icing.
Its walls were battalions of trees,
Naked, but uniformed in snow;
Like soldiers on parade,
Wearing their bearskins of crows' nests.

The barracks were pig troughs,
Lined up, ready for inspection,
Snow hanging off their curved lids
As they stood alone
In the cold field,
Rutted like a pastry cutter.

Then the roll call sounded.
A cockerel called out
His shrill alarm.
The soldiers' bearskins were alive
Once more with crows
Crowded into one tree.

All is quiet now
As my nose grows numb,
Compressed against the window.
Nothing moves in the snow.
Everything is gone
As the sun takes his fiery throne.

*Toby Driver 12 years*


All the poems quoted in this section have been written for spoken performance. The sense of audience was immediate. Already accustomed to the idea of harnessing sound to meaning, this particular project provides a salutary experience of poetry in performance. Sometimes a child revises his poem after rehearsal – re-drafting with a purpose. At other times when a child is speaking another child's poem there can be useful collaboration between writer and speaker. Above all, the writing is seen to be valued. There is response.

## 6 A Wizard of Earthsea

*A Wizard of Earthsea* is, first of all, an exciting, powerful story which children enjoy. It is also a parable of language which can form a proper basis of imaginative writing in prose and poetry. Like all parables or fables, it can be read at various levels; the most important level, however, is the story and related activities must not be tangential. (This would destroy the story's integrity by placing wrong emphases and distorting the themes.) In her essay 'Dreams Must Explain Themselves' Ursula le Guin herself says her novel is

> 'in one aspect, about the artist ... the artist as magician. The Trickster, Prospero ... Wizardry is artistry. The (novel) is then, in this sense, about art, the creative experience, the creative process.'

Certainly, *A Wizard of Earthsea* can be a powerful influence upon children's developing language awareness. It demonstrates the way in which language establishes identity, develops relationships and plays a vital part in the process of maturing. Ged, the young Mage, must face the pursuing Shadow which he himself has unleashed in the world; he must name it with his own name, and accept it as his darker self. Only then will he achieve integration and attain to maturity.

In another essay, 'This Fear of Dragons', Ursula le Guin makes this apology for fantasy:

> 'It is by such statements as "Once upon a time there was a dragon" or "In a hole in the ground there lived a hobbit" – it is by such beautiful non-facts that we fantastic human beings may arrive, in our peculiar fashion, at the truth.'

To read fantasy with children is to make no concessions to them. *A Wizard of Earthsea* will challenge and even frustrate at times; most importantly, it will give insight into the discipline of the poet's craft, the structure of his language, and identify the source of his inspiration.

The central theme of the novel is 'Naming'. This Naming emphasises the identity of the individual contained within the uniqueness of his first name. In *A Wizard of Earthsea* first names are magical, powerful, and conferred with ceremony. The boy Sparrowhawk receives his true name, Ged, at a baptism in the cold waters of the Ar. His name is known only to himself and his Namer, Ogion. It must be guarded jealously because to lose one's name into the hands of an enemy, is to surrender one's self. All this has Biblical/historical undertones and is at odds with the casual modern indifference by which first names are such common currency that they are even displayed on car windscreens, easy prey to hostile forces lurking in hedgerow or ditch.

Ged is youthful, headstrong and reckless. His energy and enthusiasm rebel against tutor Ogion's gentle, yet rigorous training. Ged wants to work spells but has to learn names before he can aspire to mastery. Then, one day Ogion teaches him the name of the plant fourfoil. Naively, the apprentice asks what use it is. Ogion answers

> 'When you know the fourfoil in all its seasons root and leaf and flower, by sight and scent and seed, then you may learn its true name, knowing its being which is more than its use. What, after all,

is the use of you, or of myself? Is Gont mountain useful, or the Open Sea?'

This is an articulation of the art of the poet. Only when we learn the true name of our subject, 'know its being', can we aspire to poetry. Moreover, we must 'know' through the senses

'by sight and scent and seed.'

Only then will the spell work, the poem say what we mean. Heather and Robin Tanner's book *Woodland Plants* complements this idea usefully and can be a legitimate digression. First, their commitment is impressive – a book started in 1939, laboured over for 42 years and finally published in 1981. Secondly, the informative text, balanced with meticulous drawings, communicates a true sense of 'knowing' by 'sight and scent and seed'. Drawings and text aspire to the truth of the creative artist. The exercise was costly.

At this point the children are able to attempt 'plant' poems, aware of the immensity of their task, yet hopeful of the potency of their craft. This is because they are working within the context of a literary/artistic experience; therein only can they find expression and release.

Heath Groundsel

Strolling through this wicker sea,
my bare feet wriggle,
as the breeze
plays with the seeds of peacock feathers.
They drift down
from the string petals,

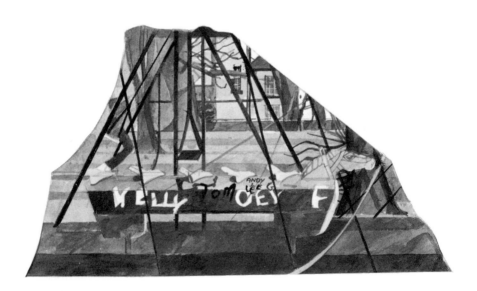

and a dancing tube,
filled with a milky sap,
bobs,
trying to loosen its tethered hold.
Serpents' tongues,
canvas covered,
green with spite,
lash out
at other plant life,
stooping below the sunset,
reflected in its territory.

*Kay Chambers  12 years*


The Dump

Dead daffodils lie
buried under mass of
tangled weed and cabbages.
Twigs intertwine, trapping
yet another fieldmouse;
whiskers twitch, apprehensively,
as a shadow menacingly
glides, distorting, over the
creature's home.
The black shape pauses
on a rotten bunch of
primroses, blotting out light
as fieldmouse scampers
away startled but safe.
Woodlice crawl, twigs
form bridges across
chasms of weed, as
falcon recedes, beaten.

Now, it is quieter than quiet,
darker than dark.

*Adam Shepherd  12 years*


Poppies

The poppies swayed,
Their bright bonnets,
spots on the field's face,
Nodding graciously
As the wind passes by.

Long stringy necks,
Fluctuating gently,
Peace and tranquillity
blowing in the breeze.

Dispersing seeds
From a baby's rattle,
Then dying from the world
To be reborn.

*Alison Wright  12 years*


Silver Birch

Birch trunk.
A slender shiny broom handle.
Silver.
Black cracks slice its skin,
Scarring the silver plated armour.
Wounded by weather.

Branches, like weak rubber tubing,
Bend in the wind,
Thin leaves flutter
Like paper emeralds above
The catkins heavy with pollen.

Soaken twigs droop over the trunk
Like the woollen threads of a wet mop.
The earth covered with
Dead leaves and twigs.
A carpet of compost.
Winter death for a new Spring.

*Anthony Collins  13 years*


Heath

Spider web branches
Flung themselves furiously at the ground
Trying to unpluck the neatly woven stitches
That had been sewn to make the heath.
Mist silently crept down,
Yet it seemed hesitant
To touch the ground
As if it might spoil the patchwork
Or be swallowed into another world.

*Julie Gilbert  13 years*

Silver Birch

A peeling bark of grey,
Infected with a chicken pox
Of knot holes.
In summer highly pollinated catkins
Camouflaged against serrated leaves.
But as Autumn draws on,
She bravely bares her branches
For Nature's sake.
And on the coming of winter
They are replaced by a cold cloak of snow.
Now there is fragile silver,
Wispy, like an old man's hair.
And he carries a walking stick
Of ants crawling up the shivery bark.
The ants crawl on
Until they reach Spring.
A new beginning,
A peeling bark of grey.

*Alison Enticknap 12 years*

Ogion's words about the fourfoil have a particular relevance for teachers today. This is a decade much concerned with 'usefulness'. Education must be relevant to industry, must be linked to the production and consumption needs of a technological society. Often the Arts may be accommodated only where they can demonstrate a dubious relevance to vocational training. Here Ogion gently questions such 'usefulness': the 'Being' of any person or thing 'is more than its use'. It is enough that it is. And all this within the context of a novel in which great deeds are enacted and a high value set on the common things of ordinary life: weatherworkers have a most practical rôle to play, binding spells make boats seaworthy, real wheatcakes are entirely preferable to meat pies which are mere illusion. Always, however, it is the wizard-artist who embodies the spirit of Earthsea. Art transcends 'usefulness' and any society which denigrates its wizard-artists loses its soul, and, paradoxically, its 'usefulness' at the same time.

Ged's precocity and the latent power within him chafe against the quiet tenor of his life with Ogion. Soon Ogion is forced to present his pupil with an ultimatum: learn to be silent with Ogion, 'the long road towards mastery,' or enrol as a pupil in the School for Wizards at Roke. Ged chooses Roke. Roke, however, selects its pupils carefully and entry is secured only when Ged is prepared to surrender his Name. Learning can take place only where there is trust and openness. Conversely, after having attained the status of Wizard, he is able to leave the school only when he asks the Doorkeeper his Name – to receive trust is an even greater responsibility and an essential part of the journey towards maturity. Here one child tries to express something about the nature of learning.

Student

Through the sun dried branches
I see the swallow fly.
Unfaltering, curving and swooping,
Bonded by instinct, in a way
Unknown.
Black across the sun,
Diving down, down,
Gliding through the hollowness,
Fringed by white
Through a gust and gone,
Remembered only by the wind
Buffeting its sharp passenger
Along.
The beauty of its being lithe and
Taunting, for what is its beauty when
Tethered?
I, the swallow,
Bound to this place,
A great cavern of stone and magic.
Warmer it gets now I have
Intruded solemnly, to be placed
In a world of learning,
Appearing more forbidding
As the ebbing tide of time
Pushes by.

*John Riches  13 years*


In this school all relates to Naming. At one point the students are sent to the
Isolate Tower where they spend their time learning long lists of names:
>'Magic consists in this, the true naming of a thing.'

The lists are endless. Language has infinite permutations and just as the wizard's
task is hopeless, so is the poet's. Nevertheless
>'A mage can control only what is near him, what he can name
>exactly and wholly.'

and the lists must be tackled. Always there is the incentive of the power that for
Ged lies:
>'like a jewel at the bottom of a dry well.'

These names are old; they have their sources deep within the culture of the people.
>'Some names have been lost over the ages, and some have been
>hidden, and some are known only to the dragons and to the Old
>Power of Earth, and some are known to no living creature; and no
>man could learn them all. For there is no end to that language.'

There is mystery and excitement in these words which express man's ultimate aspirations, aspirations embodied in all Art, and here, most particularly, in poetry – the 'Naming' art of the wizard.

The Hardic language of Earthsea derives from the 'Old Speech'. Beginnings and roots are crucial. The way in which the Hardic language has developed from the metaphors of the 'Old Speech' demonstrates and clarifies the meaning of metaphor. Just as these metaphors of the 'Old Speech' are a more vital, more powerful language than the everyday Hardic Speech, so, for us, poetry is the most direct, strongest language of all when we want to say something important. Hardic *sukien* (foam) derives from the Old Speech *suk* (feather), *inien* (sea); ie, 'foam' is 'feather of the sea'. The need for exactness and appropriateness in metaphor is immediately apparent and the basis for work in which the children invent their own list of metaphors relating to the natural world. For example:

Wind – bed of the gull
       bird's rudder
       howl of the dying wolf
       husky breath of the giant
Birds – feathered darts
Ivy – Nature's scaffolding
Snow – down of the goose
       fur of the snow seal
Thunder – clapping of the winds
Hail – peaks off mountains
Bark – skin of a dead serpent

Lists appertain to the Isolate Tower and for a short while, as they coin these metaphors, the children take up residence there. In the Isolate Tower
       'It was cold and half-dark and always silent.'
While not cold and half-dark in the classroom, there is the relaxed silence of absorbed activity. *A Wizard of Earthsea* opens with a paradox:
       'Only in silence the word,
       Only in dark the light,
       Only in dying life,
       Bright the hawk's flight
       On the empty sky.'
Part of the tension of paradox is that it can only ever be partly resolved. Here, in experiencing something of the commitment of the poet, the children sense, at an intuitive level, that somewhere there is a resolution of all opposites, a harmony which is Truth. Wizards must aspire to it in their spells; poets in their metaphors.

I have found this work can be reinforced by a digression into Riddles. Although a digression, a study of Anglo-Saxon and modern Riddles can add another dimension to the reading, rather than compromise it. This is because a Riddle is a special kind of Naming. In a Riddle the name is secret (like so many true names in *A Wizard of Earthsea*). The poet alone knows the name hidden within the Riddle; his art is to reveal it to others through metaphor and to surprise while doing so. This word study is all the more potent because it derives from our culture. The condensed form of metaphor which was the Anglo-Saxon Kenning ('whale-road' for sea etc.) makes an appropriate introduction to Kevin Crossley-Holland's translations of Riddles: 'Pen and Fingers', 'Weathercock', 'Bellows', 'Anchor' and others.

Then there are the intriguing modern puzzles of May Swenson's *Natural Songs*. Children usually guess the 'answers' correctly and in their small success is a delight in realising the likeness between dissimilars. They are surprised – but only as they engage with the text as active readers. Excitement comes through a sharing of a secret which involves this special reciprocity between reader and poet. Then the roles are reversed and the children write their own Riddles. That is, they try to reveal the whole object by naming its parts in metaphor.

Smoke

The wistful figure
Dancing and prancing on the breeze.
The grey and ghostly
Haunting the rooftops,
The spirit of the warm and beautiful.

*David Lawrence 11 years*

Pen

Light as a feather,
Going over the land leaving footprints.
One bony leg
Clambering over the hills, and jumping.
It has to be refilled
By blue rivers,
Making marks.

*Caroline Smith 10 years*

The school in Roke deals in magic. Where there is magic, there must be rules. The rules are not articulated but rather implicit within the hierarchy of Archmage Nemmerle and the nine Masters whose business it is to educate the young mages. For instance, there is the matter of Equilibrium. The world is held in delicate balance and all wizards must be responsible in the way they exercise their power. Ged learns this lesson from the Master Changer who tells him:

'A wizard's power of Changing and of Summoning can shake the balance of the World . . . It must follow knowledge and serve need. To light a candle is to cast a shadow.'

But Ged, who has wanted to change a rock into a diamond, feels dissatisfied with his Master's cautious wisdom. There is a parallel here with the Biblical story of the temptation in the Wilderness when Jesus was tempted to change a stone into bread. His refusal was a refusal to disturb the balance of the World, a respect for this Earth which transcended the gratification of his own needs. Children easily make these literary/Biblical connections and through them are able to ask questions about the special responsibilities of modern scientists to maintain the balance of our world today. There is, however, no heavily didactic purpose in *A Wizard of Earthsea*. Rather, these issues give depth to an exciting story which has all the pace to hold attention to the end. Reading a novel like this teaches more about conservation, than any amount of overt preaching. As Ursula le Guin says:

'fantasy is true'.

If the children are to assimilate and understand these basic themes of the novel, they must write and talk. One way is to adopt the role of Archmage Nemmerle and formulate rules for the school. Further, by articulating the rules, the children sometimes, unwittingly, say something about creative process. One child wrote this:

### Rules for the School at Roke

1. To form a Changing spell is to fool your sight and others.
Illusion is a mere trick to please.
2. Be humble, not proud.
3. Naming spells must be learned.
4. You must give the school power over you by giving them your true name.
5. Never summon an animal for your own practice.
6. Summon not the hawk to balance on your arm many times in a day unless need has it.
7. The spells of summoning, binding, naming, changing must be kept from normal people.
8. Summoning someone from the dead is forbidden to anyone not yet knowing the consequences which might befall him.
9. Illusion is like your shoe. It grows bigger as you grow bigger. Do not attempt an Illusion shown to you by an older apprentice, only ones taught to you by the Master Hand.
10. Learn weather working from the Master Windkey only.
11. Learn the use of herbs from the Master Herbal only. Learn not these arts from any other pupil in the school.
12. Summon a being only by its true name.
13. Duels with magic are strictly forbidden.
14. Spite not your fellow apprentice, work well and enjoy his company.

Life in Roke is not always serious. The students are encouraged to play with and enjoy illusion. Although their work is rigorous and demanding, they find joy in it. A humourless Wizard would be a weak Wizard; a humourless poet, an ineffectual poet.

The chapter 'Iffish' provides another opportunity for legitimate digression. Vetch, Ged's great friend, has a sister Yarrow. Yarrow has no power but is curious. She asks Ged

'What other great powers are there beside the light?'

Ged replies

'It is no secret. All power is one in source and end . . . My name and yours, and the true name of the sun, or a spring of water, or an unborn child, all are syllables of the great word that is very slowly spoken by the shining of the stars. There is no other power. No other name.'

Again, this is to talk of our sources. And our own culture has the appropriate symbols:

'In the beginning was the Word.'

Within this literary experience these words have a special meaning for those concerned with the power of language. Richard Church, in his autobiography *Over the Bridge*, writes of their devastating effect when, as a boy in the classroom, he stumbled across them accidentally.

'I saw a new skyline defined. It was a landscape in which objects and words were fused. All was one, with the word as the verbal reality brought to material life by Mind, by man. It was therefore the very obvious, tangible presence of the Creator . . . I received a philosophy which I have never lost, a working faith in the oneness of all life . . . Everything was now contained for me, in the power of the Word.'

Richard Church himself admits that his response was over-literal, but, nevertheless, is quite sure of the authenticity of the experience. While it is unlikely that any of our children will have a Damascene literary experience of this kind, it is possible, that by considering our beginnings, they will make another of those connections within their culture and take another step on the road to language awareness. For example, our own Genesis story of creation read alongside some of the other great creation myths of the world, such as the Indian 'Shatarupa' provides a literary experience through which their understanding of the 'Word', as defined in *A Wizard of Earthsea*, is confirmed and deepened.

It is the Mage Ogion who defines the need for each person to attempt to come to terms with his beginnings if he is to grow to full maturity.

'a man would know the end he goes to, but he cannot know it if he does not turn, and return to his beginnings and hold that beginning in his being.'

For us this is most possible within the structure of the received literary forms which are our particular heritage. We must know the great Creation myths of the World – our own especially. They are true in a special way; they embody each person's separate attempt to come to terms with his beginnings in order that he might know his end.

The children's attempts to articulate these beginnings must seem both audacious and stumbling within this context. They can be, nevertheless, necessary and authentic stages of language growth.


The Creation of the World

A child plays with his small red, blue and yellow ball. He throws it against the wall again and again and it rebounds every time like a piece of elastic springing back into place.

Now he kicks his ball high into the air. It falls straight down to land at his feet and again rebounds into the sky. He kicks it again. This time it does not fall at his feet but lands in a small stream.

It turns, twists and spins around, a small globe in the middle of a water universe.

The stones and pebbles, browns and blacks and whites mixed together are tiny planets around the small world. Slowly the current spins it around down the river of eternity.

A water lily for a sun. And the moon? A pure white feather, bent like a crescent, floats downstream.

The microbes in the water stick to the globe to form mindless beasts to live on this world in the infancy of its existence.


The End of the World

As the world drifts downstream it is punctured by the sharp edge of a flint. Now the small and colourful ball is twisted and wrinkled.

The little boy picks it up and slowly, sorrowfully, tears trickle down his cheeks. But his caring mother comforts him and from behind her back produces another blue, red and yellow ball.


*Samantha Ellis 13 years*


Creation

Imagine . . .
Nothingness, blackness, non-life.
A single spark, light, as a
Moon starts a sun glowing,
Growing, winning its body by
A timeless dawn, the Alpha of
Omega, the grain of a mountain.
A world.
A spawn, an aspiring life roots
And begins. A movement.
The rustle, the learning spreads
As does the light.
It grows, multiplies;
Maybe a fish inheriting a past,
An eel or salmon but always
Life. Light.

*John Riches 13 years*

Central to the novel is the search for one hidden name – the name of the Shadow unleashed by Ged. Until he can name the Shadow, it will roam Earthsea intent on working great evil, perhaps through Ged himself. The turning-point comes when Ged, refusing to run any longer, determines to hunt down his enemy and face it. Throughout, we have known the Shadow's name is a character in the novel and as the climax builds to the final confrontation, children speculate about its identity. Then comes the moment Ged and the Shadow speak the same name:

> 'Aloud and clearly . . . Ged spoke the Shadow's name, and in the same moment the Shadow spoke without lips or tongue, saying the same word: "Ged". And the two voices were one voice.'

This is the moment of integration.

> 'Naming the shadow of his death with his own name, (Ged) had made himself whole: a man, who, knowing his whole true self cannot be used or possessed by any power other than himself, and whose life therefore is lived for life's sake and never in the service of ruin, or pain, or hatred, or the dark.'

And so, in naming and recognising the Shadow, Ged faces his darker self and in acknowledging this side of his nature attains to self-knowledge and freedom. He grows up. Ursula le Guin says in 'Dreams Must Explain Themselves'

> 'The most childish thing about *A Wizard of Earthsea*, I expect, is its subject: coming of age.'

She enlarges on this theme in 'This Fear of Dragons':

> 'maturity is not an outgrowing, but a growing up . . . an adult is not a dead child, but a child who survived.'

By that criterion, many never attain to maturity. It is teachers' business at least to aspire to this for themselves and their pupils. Moreover, it is through developing language awareness, making the necessary literary connections, that self-awareness grows, develops into self-acceptance. Only then can we turn outward – articulate, expressive, whole.

Finally, Ursula le Guin's apology for fantasy (from 'This Fear of Dragons'). It is also, of course, an apology for English as a literature-based Arts subject in our schools.

> 'For fantasy is true, of course. It isn't factual but it is true. Children know that. Adults know it too, and that is precisely why many of them are afraid of fantasy. They know that its truth challenges, even threatens, all that is false, all that is phony, unnecessary, and trivial in the life they have let themselves be forced into living. They are afraid of dragons because they are afraid of freedom.'

## 7 The Poem and the Story

The following poems stand well on their own with the minimum of background explanation. Because they are poems about people, for the most part, they arise out of anecdote. We all share a natural curiosity about people, sometimes expressed through unstructured gossip, occasionally through structured story, and, rarely, through the discipline and craft of poetry. Any encounter with a person is important because it may initiate a relationship, and a relationship implies a 'knowing'. We learn to 'know' a person only in part by looking; a poem comprising a list of physical details, however finely perceived and sensitively selected, may well end up by being clinical and inhuman. There must be an attempt to capture something of the mystery of human personality. Most of the following poems attempt this through concrete, physical imagery related to a specific happening. 'Old Grandma' by Gail Bloomfield, for instance, was written a year after she had experienced a fleeting encounter with a very old woman. The poem, however, became possible only after reading extracts from Laurie Lee's *Cider with Rosie* and, in particular, Elizabeth Jennings, 'My Grandmother'. These readings gave meaning and importance to Gail's seemingly trivial holiday encounter. Again, through making the necessary literary connections within her own experience she was enabled to articulate her meeting with an old woman she had never met before and, probably, will never see again. Her words, I feel, say something new about the general condition of old age through a moment of empathy with that one old person.

Old Grandma

Her skin clung to the oldness
Of her hand like rose petals
Clothed in water.
She folded my hand in hers
And patted it softly.

She looked at me with the lustre of a diamond
In each eye.
Her hair was twined back into
A grey bun, swerving and
Curving its way round
Like soft smoke.

Her eyes wandered with thoughts
And stared at me.

I bent forward and kissed her wrinkled cheek.
It was like kissing clay,
All cold and soft.

I took a deep breath and smelled
Mint humbugs and golden fudges.

I felt saddened by the way she moved
Like a clock winding down,
Getting slower.
      POOR old GRANDMA.

*Gail Bloomfield 13 years*

The following poem, 'Gran' by Gregory Block, shows a thirteen year old re-living an encounter made at seven years old. Gregory made this visit with his mother and the poem, written six years later, re-captures the fine perceptions of the small child's memory in images like
      'A cup of tea on the bedside table,
      As cold as winter.'
On the other hand, there is the conscious detachment of the young adult in the objective first line:
      'Just a timid seven-year-old;'
For his mother there was the sudden shock of realisation as a lost memory returned. For all of us there is delight and recognition in words like
      'Always I had cream sherry and a Rich Tea biscuit;'
which contain something of our common experience of old age. So often children have this special access to past events which they have apprehended with a peculiarly poetic sharpness. At seven Gregory had neither the language nor the self-consciousness to articulate the experience; at thirteen he had both and the poem was written.


Gran

Just a timid seven-year-old;
Gran never moved from that musty bed,
Restricted,
As if she had spent a lifetime or more lying
    under those covers.
94 colossal years hung by a thread.
I, her great grandchild, just one of many others.
The perfect setting,
Her daughter, 64, now ageing,
And a budgie swearing and screaming.
Always I had cream sherry and a Rich Tea biscuit;
Lacy white curtains sieved the sun,
As we went in twos to see her;
Her fragile voice would scrape our ears,
Although she couldn't see us.
A cup of tea on the bedside table,
As cold as winter.

Dead,
Just like Gran.

*Gregory Block  13 years*


Similarly, the following poems have 'story' backgrounds and need no further
introduction.


Beth and the Jet

She was born on a still but rainy night.
When she was a week old,
She was still and quiet,
Like a bud just opened.
She lay in mother's arms,
As if waiting for something unknown.
Then, that something came:
A jet flew over,
Making the door rattle,
And making the calendar fall to the floor.
Heard?
Maybe, but never seen.
All eyes were on Beth.
She had stopped smiling.
She had stopped moving.
Everyone was frozen,
As if packed in ice.
Then she started crying,
But small choked sobs,
Pausing . . .
Then starting once more.
I left the room.
I will never forget.

*Jude Fitzgerald  11 years*


Old Woman

Last week's crossword discarded,
A morning's hard labour.
Her coffee, the colour
Of her dentures,
Cheek bones jutting out
Like the hind of a jersey.

## 8 Water

This topic may be introduced with readings of two 'water' poems by Seamus Heaney which I have found work well with twelve to thirteen year olds. It is commonly argued that to ask a child to write a poem immediately after having read one is to debase the original work and, more importantly, to preclude enjoyment. I have found, however, that it is immediately after having made a literary connection within a text that a child finds that he has something worthwhile to say. Again, it is a matter of excitement. Recognitions are exciting and need articulating. The moment of identification can become an expressive moment if an area of experience has been defined in a new and surprising way.

The first poem, 'Personal Helicon', is a return to the childhood fascination with water. This is to return us, through the minutiae of the memories, to our own beginnings. First, there is the specific naming of 'pumps', 'buckets', 'windlasses' – concrete, unadorned 'naming'. Then, the hint of mystery, the sinister undertone in 'dark drop', 'trapped sky'. The poem is heavily sensuous and therefore deliberately evocative. There is a dwelling on the smells, the sounds, the textures:

> 'the smells
> Of waterweed, fungus and dank moss . . .
> I savoured the rich crash when a bucket
> Plummeted down at the end of a rope . . .'

Most importantly, echoes and reflections run throughout. To a child, an echo or reflection is a fascinating affirmation of self, almost an image of the self-knowledge which lies tantalisingly just around the corner. It is, above all, a matter for play and experiment; sometimes, as in stanza 4, for fearful experiment.

> 'And one (well)
> Was scaresome for there, out of ferns and tall
> Foxgloves, a rat slapped across my reflection.'

Foxgloves are poisonous; there is also the aggressive assonance of 'rat slapped'. And our vulnerable, curious self is threatened. The quest for knowledge of the world and our own place in it is a dangerous quest. Similarly, the work of the poet in stanza 5 is no less fearful, needs no less temerity. The childish play and experiment is over and now

> 'I rhyme
> To see myself, to set the darkness echoing.'

These twelve to thirteen year olds are at a moment in their lives when they are particularly receptive to this poem. They have a foot in both worlds. They still play and experiment in an entirely childlike way but they are also becoming young adults, capable of the poetic detachment which will set their own darkness echoing. They have, at the same time, the poet's and the child's apprehension of 'reflection'. Looking at a reflection is introspective; there must now be a turning outwards, if a poem is to be written. The inevitable question follows: where is your own 'Personal Helicon'? This question is an especially authentic starting point for children's writing. The connection with the Greek Muses confers a special importance on the task. There is no point in writing about anything unless it is important (although paradoxically, of course, it can be only the act of writing which makes a matter of this kind important). Thereby the writer attains to self-respect as well as self-knowledge.

Read alongside this poem, 'Death of a Naturalist' adds another dimension. Again the poet returns to childhood and so his subject is easily accessible to children. In rank, sensuous imagery Seamus Heaney paints a picture of the festering flax dam and his boyhood fascination with:

'the warm thick slobber
Of frogspawn that grew like clotted water.'

Then there is the cosy familiarity of the classroom world where Nature is contained within jam jars and Miss Walls reduces all to Nursery dimensions.

'Miss Walls would tell us how
The daddy frog was called a bullfrog
And how he croaked and the mammy frog
Laid hundreds of little eggs and this was
Frogspawn.'

There is the comfortable folklore of

'You could tell the weather by frogs too
For they were yellow in the sun and brown
In rain.'

Then the conversational rhythm breaks. There is the ominous, heavy tread of syllables in

'Then one hot day when fields were rank'

and we come upon the tough, primitive reality which is poetry. Miss Walls' jam jar of sentimentality cracks – her cosy classroom world plays the boy false when he is confronted by the angry, invading frogs:

'their loose necks pulsed like sails. Some hopped.
The slap and plop were obscene threats. Some sat
Poised like mud grenades, their blunt heads farting.'

And the 'naturalist' within the little boy dies as he sickens, turns and runs.

Obviously much remains to be said about both these poems but these are readings for children, designed only to send them back to their own experience with a sense of discovery and importance. Each of the following poems was written after these two readings. In no way do they 'copy' Seamus Heaney (that would indeed be to debase his work). Rather, the professional poet has helped them to re-visit a watery place and recapture its atmosphere through the feelings associated with it.


The Terrapin

His tortoise-shell back, a barnacle
Clutching at the painted algae.
His pipe-cleaner neck rigid,
His lonely head shunts to one side, staring into nothing,
The lamp-lit world empty without his shy companion.
His grim features seem to say,
'Where's my friend? Where's my brother?'

He rolls into the water
And attacks his reflection in the glass.
As the gravel swirls, sand storms arise –
Now the tank is a smoke sheet, a creeping fog.
Then – out of the mist, a prehistoric fossil
   clambers to its rock
To wait alone for its own end.

*Matthew Shepherd 11 years*

River Blyth

In the summer I waded the Blyth.
Slipping on muddy flints,
I travelled the length of the river.
At one point,
Baby eels sucked at my toes
And tiny water spiders secretly
Hid between specks of sand.

On and on
The soft mud
Grudgingly let my walking stick
Sink into its oozy layers.

Then – a reed laced with dirt
Where a kingfisher
Dashed nearby into
The murky below
And caught a minnow.

On under the bridge
Where nothing grew,
Except slippery slime.
Flounders scudded
As I kicked duckweed.

I clambered up the sun-baked river bank.
Pieces of earth
Crumbled like a biscuit
Into the water below.
Satisfied,
I made my way home.

*Matthew Watson 13 years*

## Our Pond

In one corner,
under the paving,
lives a grass snake;
he looks like a creased-up old drinking straw
and swims around
eating the pondskaters,
scraps of tinfoil,
frail and easily broken.

Newts live in that pond;
they are lazy,
sun-worshipping sticks;
Any movement,
and each stick finds legs and dashes to safety.

The water snail,
living in hermit fashion,
and coated with algae,
wants only the peace and quiet to eat his meal.

The goldfish,
a lazy mass of flesh poised between life and death,
is still like a picture.

Our pond is a natural habitat;
man, an outsider:
Please leave Nature at work.

*Russell Wood 12 years*


## The River

The clear, slow-running river
is a two-way mirror.
Fish stare up at me
through my reflection.

A kingfisher,
a spectrum of colours,
perched on an overhanging tree,
studies the still waters,
its beak a sharpened spear-head.
A silver torpedo
fins past.
A flash of blue spark,
a dart in the bull's-eye.

An orange-peel sunset
lies on the water.
Coke cans and
brown crisp packets
bob up and down like plastic ducks
on the scarlet mirror.
A running stream of warm blood.

As I stand back, knee-deep
in the deathly silence,
only the ripples slapping
against my boots,
fear rises in my throat,
a weird feeling.
Through the nettles and brambles
I pull my boots
from the black oozing mud –
and run.

*Malcolm Goodwin  13 years*


Tree Collection

Rainwater,
Collected in the stump of a three-way tree,
Ripples
Like a transparent blanket
Shaken between two people;
Only no dust is blown up.
Tiny fragments of bark falling,
Like melted icicles,
Gently slide into the water.
The specks rock back and forth, like a cradle,
As they slowly sink down.
As the wind drops,
An autumn leaf floats on the surface,
Its once crispy skin,
Soggy,
Like clothes soaking in the kitchen sink.
A beetle comes crawling down the trunk,
As if stalking a life or death prey.
A metallic spectrum
On its jet black back
Glitters in the sun.
I listen hard;
The wind is rustling the first leaves of spring,
A mother soothing her baby.

No other sound;
The whole world seems to be silent for me,
Just how it should be,
As I gaze into my miniature universe.

*Lara Mair 10 years*


Stillness

The water is still,
Except for a trickle of breeze
Through the curving willows.
A piece of crust
Left by the flustering ducks,
Drifts gently out
Like a graceful swan.
Mud stirs,
And the crust is suddenly immersed
In a battle of swirls and swells.
They stop.
And a fanned out fin
Breaks the surface.
Then comes a telescopic mouth,
And with a suck and a gargle
The crust is gone with the great carp
To the decaying bottom.
An angler whips his fine tackle
Out to the quivering reeds,
While a timid water-vole
Scurries through the overhanging grass
And into the water.
His ripples die
And sink.
The water is still.

*Jamie MacDonald 12 years*


That Pond!

Swiftly gliding about,
Suddenly tipping up a little,
The water making a V shape after the boat.
We were screaming for joy.
Then, turning around and heading for the shore,
Elizabeth gradually stepped out.
I wanted to go with her,
Like a little child wanting to go with her mother.

I was about to step when . . .
Elizabeth shouted, 'Hang on!'
Too late . . .
I fell in.
Haah!
Help!
Splashing about.
The taste of the slimy dirty water,
The ducks flying out of the way,
Their wings spread,
And shouting that they had been disturbed.
Elizabeth slowly hauled me out.
Standing on the shore dripping wet,
The squelchy feeling of water in my boots,
Like a soggy squelchy jellyfish.
I ran home
And went into my bedroom crying.
Then – feeling of clothes
And warm air around me.
I felt glad to be at home –
But
That pond!

*Rosalind Roberts 11 years*

Canal

Jumping on the stone slabs,
I balance on one leg.
I wobble,
    stumble,
        then fall.
It is cold.
My head goes under and I cannot see.
The thick surface reflects the sun,
And looks like tinted glass.
The wall of the canal is covered
With a tapestry of slime,
Wet leaves woven together with hair.
My shoe comes off
And my foot strokes the bottom;
The mud is warm to my toes
And floats to the surface, like strands of smoke.
Air bubbles, too, rise like transparent balloons,
Only to pop at the surface.
And water floods through my clothes
And weighs me down.

Kicking and spluttering,
I rise to the surface, hold my breath,
And sink back down again.
Then up like a yo-yo.
I am hauled to land like a captured fish.
But now I can breathe.
The water is still
But a murky patch pollutes the dank surface
And swirls in endless patterns
To settle on the bottom, in my lost shoe.

*Sally Clifton  12 years*


A return to some of the 'sea' prose pieces in the Journal of Gerard Manley Hopkins was the starting point of some 'sea' poetry linked to the 'water' theme. Again, the imagery demonstrates the individuality of the response;
    'And there are channels,
    Like the veins of a clipped pony's neck'
could be written only by a child who has worked with horses and has made a particularly arresting connection with another area of her experience – the seashore. The image is new, surprising, and was released through a close reading of some prose pieces by Gerard Manley Hopkins. These pieces made her own experience important and worth writing about.

Seaside Show

Sea surf trickles;
Water ripples scurry to the sand,
Leaving spidery channels
Like a small child's writing.
Scuffing shoes.
One stone,
Speckled like a thrush's breast.
A hidden vacuum sucks at my boot.
A seagull screams overhead,
Protesting it seems.
I scrape a stone along the sand
And there are channels
Like the veins of a clipped pony's neck.
Pom-pom creatures bristle,
Red silk waves.
Tentacles plunge;
And then all is calm.
Only the gentle splish splash cf the sea.

*Ruth Hooton  12 years*

## Washed Up

A yard of fishing net,
torn rope hugging the silt,
an empty oil drum beating
to the sound of waves.
Jellyfish, stodgy cake mix,
rotting in the sun.

A bar of driftwood
scrawls tiny ditches
on the sand;
the brine seeps
into caves in the wood
and flakes off splinters
on to the moist sand.

An oil-sodden seagull
is tarred to pebbles
and is dead as a wall.
Its liquorice body ruffles
in the bite of the wind.

Bulbs of seaweed
scratch against golden sand
and quiver as the tide nears,
spewing out froth as it comes.
The seaweed disappears
under a mass of water once more.

The tide ebbs
and the treasure trove of debris
moves out to the deeps,
again.

*Matthew Goddard  13 years*


## Rock Pool

Rock pool, rock pool,
See the sand guzzle
The sour sea.
Each drip of water,
Tasteless and dry.
A swirl of sand rubs
Between my toes,
Worms wriggling.

Faint echoes of ships' horns
Blowing
And the rock pools humming.
A small crab,
Its legs long, thin.
Its eyes,
Sizes of melon pips.
I touch the crab's shell.
Hard but breakable,
It looks like a soft green lily top.
A pebble lies crushed,
Smashed against the tide's
Pestle and mortar,
And now
The pebbles are the sands.

*Michelle Saunders 13 years*

Story can also be a sound basis for poetry writing. Obviously the story must be sufficiently well known for the poem to read well out of context. An excellent source of such stories is the Bible. The two 'watery' stories 'Noah's Ark' and 'Moses in the Bulrushes' were the background for the poems which follow. As with the Christmas writing, the aim was to give an old story new relevance and impact. These two stories seem less likely to evoke stereotyped images, perhaps because we do not celebrate them. Nevertheless, they are deeply woven into our culture and the kind of story we feel we always knew. A good starting point for the 'Noah' story is Judith Nicholls' 'Japheth's Notes – A Fragment'. The title itself asserts a new reality, while the images are sensuous and conceived within the terms of the writer's experience – so they make the story new.

'First waterdrops
on father's upturned head,
dew on a web of thinning hair . . .
Nostrils sharp with gopher wood and pitch.'

This is, above all, an attempt to answer the question 'What was it really like?' This is a challenge to the imagination and, again, it can be met only within the writer's memory. Indeed it is only as the old story makes connections within the experience of each generation that it works as a story. A poem about that story must arise out of those personal connections. Moreover, the Ark is a particularly appropriate subject for poetry as it is itself a poetic symbol. Each animal aboard the ark was one particular creature which had attained universality. The cows, for example, were two unique creatures which nevertheless represented all cows everywhere. This idea builds on and extends the work done on the children's 'Thought-Creature' poems. It forms for them another layer of poetic experience.

Noah's Ark

The cow's body
like a map,
the giraffe's neck
like a ladder.
The monkey's ears
ready to take off.
And Noah's print
in cow's dung
like a big black hole
drying fast.
The spiders in the corner
spinning their
riches of wet pearls.
The elephant wrinkled
like a closed-up hand.
The parrot talking,
performing its act.
The apes' holloas
like foghorns.

While outside
the sea is drowning
and the ark riding its waves.

*Emma Smith  13 years*

The Great Flood

The meadow now a painter's palette;
Bulrushes, escaped bristles from a brush,
Drowning in paint, drowning in water.
A blind-witted hedgehog trundles to its death,
Sinks, leaving tips of spikes as floating gold dust.

A tree's roots turn into dead man's fingers,
Wilting to soft decaying pulp.
Like a lost child, a starling,
Clenching to a rock,
Cries out to the sky.
For help?

The meadow is now the weighted wings
Of a frail butterfly;
Straining with no energy,
Straining to keep above the surface.

The butterfly sinks as the water rises.

*Gail Bloomfield 13 years*


Noah's Ark

The ark, the one and only.
Stories, pictures . . . can't imagine how big it really was . . .
How terrifying that first raindrop that fell,
The first haynet which was filled
Full of sweet-smelling hay,
Caught in our terrified minds like smoke.
The loneliness of a cow, missing her calf,
Stands desolated in a corner.
Pigs grunt, groan;
They do not show their loneliness; their hearts are strong.
I walk to the stall. A muzzle gathers on my hand.
Then . . . they all sleep.

When that first and last raindrop fell . . .
How wonderful to have seen through that terrible storm.
Stories, pictures . . . can't imagine how bad
    it really was . . .
How wonderful that last raindrop that fell,
The last haynet filled.

*Sarah Wright 12 years*

Fate

Mud rises like a chiffon scarf
dancing with green slime partners;
a smell of sickness.
A tarred basket made from reeds.
Containing what?

I peer in and see a bundle,
two dark eyes peering into a forest of bulrushes
and a mouth opening and shutting
while the body struggles,
restless in the bands of linen.
The water settles.
But the dying and killing
Never stop.

*Caroline English  13 years*


The Ark

I am the ant,
The ant who boarded the world
In fright at the first drop of rain
That could kill me.
I am the ant.
My memory reflects in outside worlds
Of sweetmint air.
Now,
The smell of sweat and dung decayed.
My small body hides
Where an elephant stamped impatiently
And where a man crouched under creaking bows,
Clasped hands together and prayed.
A drop of rain
And my unbelief surrenders.
And then the motion of sadness;
The rank smell of fresh gopher wood fills me.
Yet worse –
My tiny nostrils sense stricken panic
From the outside world.
The stretch of water is endless
And already
Bodies of black and white rhinos,
Bloated with water,

Clot the surface
And a layer of insects smothers,
A covering for the already dead.
I crawl inside
And sit in a crevice
Watching the destruction
While forty days and nights pass on.
Then the dove gives thanks:
The world,
Two of each,
Will live on.

*Charlotte Hawthorn 13 years*

# 9 'Natural Selections': A World Wildlife Fund Project

In 1986 one of the most rewarding activities for the children of Halesworth Middle School was participation in the World Wildlife Fund Children's Poetry Writing Competition organised in association with the Poetry Society. Schools were invited to submit anthologies called 'Natural Selections' in which, through creative writing, their pupils explored their feelings about environmental change. This could be natural change brought about by, for example, light, seasons, wind, or change brought about by human activity, such as building, pollution, traffic movement or the destruction of wild places. The aim was 'to encourage young people to observe carefully and critically and help them to develop a greater personal awareness of their world and to reflect on what they see or hear'. The key word is 'reflect'. Most of us are unreflecting about our immediate environment because we take it for granted. To write a poem is a disturbing experience; that is, if the poem is to disturb as it should. First the poet must know that it is impossible to say exactly what he means. Secondly, he must reconcile this knowledge with a genuine attempt to find the right words. John Moat and John Fairfax in *The Way to Write* speak of literature as the celebration of an encounter. Encounters are disturbing because they initiate a relationship. When we ask children to write poetry about their environment, they will enter a relationship from which they will emerge disturbed. They will ask questions and expect answers.

After judging this competition, Ted Hughes wrote

> 'One thing that did strike me. The knowledge that our natural surroundings are now utterly polluted, poisoned, and to a great extent ruined, is a basic awareness of all these children. They seem to know it in their bones, as a sort of shared nightmare fact of existence. As they grow up, they won't have to be persuaded about what needs doing. There seems to me a great reservoir of hope in this sort of early understanding.'

As a teacher, the key words here for me are 'know it in their bones'. An English teacher does not deal in a body of knowledge which is unknown to the child; he deals with what is already known. If it is not already known it cannot be the subject of imaginative writing. Further, it has been said many times that we know what we think only as we try to write it down. In this case, through the very act of writing the poetry, the children came to realise what was already 'in their bones'. If it had not been there they could not have written with conviction. The poems they wrote made the implicit explicit and gave intuitive feelings external reality. And that reality disturbed. It disturbed the writer and the reader.

A poem written about a polluted river crystallises the writer's response. As he attempts to 'name' the river, he grows to know it and then to care about it. The poem is an affirmation of both the writer's identity and the river's. For a moment they share a mutual dependence – an encounter has grown into a relationship which implies a responsibility. The aesthetic experience of writing sharpens and focuses the moral issues more effectively than any amount of didactic teaching on care for the environment. It is no accident that much of the World Wildlife education programme concentrates on the arts in general. All this, unhappily, is against the tide of popular feeling today. Peter Abbs sums this up most coherently in these words:

> 'when we inspect the society about us . . . we find an objective materialism which has lost connection with the deep needs of the psyche . . . We find everywhere human life disconnected from its sources and subservient to the two great impersonal forces of Production and Consumption.'

As teachers we must guard and foster the expressive disciplines through which these 'deep needs of the psyche' are fulfilled. Much of the writing in the 'Natural Selections' anthologies shows children making those essential connections with the sources of human life and, certainly, as Ted Hughes has said, these poems are 'a great reservoir of hope for the future'.

It has been my privilege to read the anthologies submitted by the finalists in this competition. In most schools the work was absorbed naturally into the curriculum as an extension of projects already undertaken. At Halesworth, for instance, I found the anthology was simply a focused application of the principles already outlined in previous chapters. Certainly, the project became a search for the extraordinary within the familiar, a search in which we tried to look at our world as though for the first time. Now the sense of audience was immediate. Out there, someone was going to listen with a special attentiveness.

When country children write about the country, their approach is on the one hand, unsentimental and realistic – containing the potential of direct, vital writing. On the other hand, they may look without seeing, know without realising. Our anthology fell into four sections: 'Weather and Seasons', 'Time', 'Man' (pollution) and 'Illusions'. The 'Time' section was a study of Dunwich, a Suffolk coastal village, which had once been a thriving city comprising nine parish churches and a busy harbour. Over the centuries the sea has eaten at the coastline until today all that is left is a small village and one last gravestone from the last church, All Saints. In order to write, the children had to remember past visits there and then select and pattern details of those memories. The historical facts were already well known to them. Writing poetry imposed constraints on that knowledge and required them to realise what was known and then to work within the discipline of the poet's craft. Always the emphasis was on individual perception and the potential within each child to find the arresting image which would surprise by its truthfulness.

Dunwich

The sea creeps towards the cliffs,
Foaming at the mouth.
A savage, eating at the frayed edges of age.
The cliffs and the houses, tumbling day after day,
Are a special morsel.
Soon, soon Dunwich will be gone.

Cliffs, sandy and drawn, shift down,
Bringing tufts of grass, fences, and those graves
    of people forgotten,
It swallows.
Graves end as drift stones and fragments of wood,
As age sucks away debris of many tides, yet spilling more.
Creaming waves, lashed to fury, thunder against
Cliffs, resisting and sandy.
Then, the sea draws away, edging backwards, content,
No longer hungry,
Leaving wet ribbed sand
Where cradles of shingle hold pools of water
And skeletons of left over baby crabs.
Today bells chime in that sea, calling us to church,
Echoes of that lost Dunwich.

*Tracey Aldridge  12 years*

Dunwich

Trees, heaved upon the rocky cliffs,
Hold on
As the sea sculptures the land.
Memories form.
A seagull hovers, an old man's hand,
Shaking.
Sand collides with twigs, leaves
And a crumbling splinter of old graveyards.
Bells beneath the sea ring,
As fish swim through towers and windows of a rusty town.
As winter comes the cliffs are frosted:
Seaweed fingers, bony, old, carve into the cliffs.
Today a fisherman sits,
Patiently waiting for a catch,
As, punched and pulled by the wind's force,
    the cliffs crumble.
Standing today,
Fallen tomorrow.

*Caroline Ward  13 years*


Through all sections our preoccupation was, again, those words of George Tardios:

    'The world is troubled
    With a lack of looking.'

We tried to look, find words for what we saw, and then ask questions. Gradually the children began to 'know' aspects of their environment in the poetic sense. With that knowledge came strong feelings. The following poem, written for the 'Seasons' section is, most of all, a celebration of the natural patterns of seasonal change in the Suffolk countryside.

Seasons' Change

In autumn
A peaceful curtain is drawn.
Migrating birds fly south with the sun.
Leaves drop like stitches
And form a feathery carpet.
The stench of a mouldy apple sifts through the trees.
A dying wasp drones,
But all too soon winter attacks.

This cold-blooded beast
Has whitewashed the world
And chalk dusty clouds are opening,
Ice needles threaded
By white cotton snow.
Frost embroidered windows
Scrape woollen gloves.
Snow melts and puddles form.

A wet dishcloth drops
And spring makes silk from yarn.
The sun rises and days expand.
Tree blossom blooms,
A pink satin cloak.
Rosebuds pop
And at last summer is here.

Lace dragonflies fly
Over blue shiny ponds.
Cottonwool bees
Buzz freely off flowers,
Bearing nectar of gold.
The shady blanket
Under green trees so tall.
The peaceful curtain draws once more
And autumn prevails.

*Matthew Booley 11 years*

Through participation in this national project, these children began, at least, to take their surroundings less for granted; some developed a new appreciation and concern. Moreover there was a day of celebration when a representative from the World Wildlife Fund came to present the award. Nine other schools across the country shared in this celebration. The writers in these schools had something important to say and had made people listen.

Many entries concentrated on particular local issues. A Newton Mearns school, Crookfur Primary, for example, were especially concerned about the destruction of their village and surrounding farms to make way for housing estates and a modern shopping centre. Particularly encouraging is teacher Marion Howie's description of how the children's awareness of the local problem developed into a general concern for wider environmental issues. Their group poem 'The Old Village Is Gone' won the individual award in the five to nine-year-old section. Written on reading an interview with Mr Tom Craig, resident of Mearns, who felt bitter that his village should be destroyed when nearby Eaglesham was conserved, it captures the old man's sadness as his world changes around him.


The Old Village is Gone

'They didn't have to put it there,' the old man said.
His heart was heavy and his eyes were sad.
The village and the house where he was born,
The cobblestones he played on as a lad.

The baker where he bought his early rolls,
And broken bannocks were a special treat.
The butcher where his mother bought her beef,
Cleaver in hand and sawdust at his feet.

The grocer with his rounds of fresh-made cheese,
And tins of biscuits open on the shelves.
Weighing the coffee, scooping up the tea.
For here you didn't have to help yourselves.

But best of all, the Jenny a' Things shop
Where children pressed their noses on the glass,
Crammed to the sill with beads and mugs and toys,
Socks and laces, ornaments of brass.

'They didn't have to put it there,' he said,
'I know a village not too far away
With *Conservation Village – Please Take Care!*
I was betrayed and banished on that day
They took my home away.
They didn't have to put it there!'

*Primary Six 9–10 years*
*Crookfur Primary School*
*Newton Mearns, Glasgow*

Priorswood Primary School in Taunton submitted a fully documented account of their successful fight to restore a stream to their school grounds. These eight and nine year olds wrote to Taunton Deane Borough Council and the Wessex Water Authority and asked why their stream had stopped flowing. After a fifteen-month campaign the Council took action and the stream flowed again. Their story of one Willow tree which died, they thought, through lack of water is especially poignant and even has undertones of Wordsworth's 'Imitations of Immortality from Recollections of Early Childhood':

> 'But there's a Tree, of many, one,
> A single field which I have looked upon,
> Both of them speak of something that is gone.'

For these children, the Willow Tree had indeed gone but they remain in full possession of 'the glory and the dream'.


Streams

Ripples and patterns are the stream,
A little waterfall making bubbles,
The waterfall starts dipping.
The sound is like taps dripping.

Grass is floating under and over.
Looks like pebbles are moving side to side
But it's ripples doing all this
With help of the sun.

*Nicholas Glover 8 years*
*Priorswood Primary School*
*Taunton*


Gardens were the issue of St Thomas More Roman Catholic Primary School in London. Teacher Henrietta Kightly explains that in order to extend their limited playing area, this urban school has lost its garden. So often environmental problems are matters of delicate compromise rather than clearcut issues of right and wrong. For one child his feelings of grief at his father's death were externalised in his observations of subsequent change in his own garden. Our surroundings are deeply interwoven into the tapestry of our lives and the images in his poem are small approximations to the changes in his family.


Our Garden

The flowers standing tall and to attention,
The lawn new mown and glad to be alive,
The rambling rose that longs to have a mention,
And me with my dad standing by my side.

The garden bench brand new and slightly awkward,
With long grass creeping round its new-found legs,
The garden seats so cold and uninviting,
And my dad lying very ill in bed.

The garden like a jungle that surrounds us
With choking weeds of cancer that will spread
Across the lawn that fights for its existence.
And I'm alone because my dad is dead.

*Edward Martin 11 years*
*St Thomas More RC Primary School*
*London*

Manor Road County Primary School in Clayton-Le-Woods, Chorley is on the
fringe of the vast building programme undertaken by the Lancashire New Town
Development Corporation. Teacher Valerie Reddecliffe writes this of the
upheaval in their lives:

> 'Naturally the children have been very critical of the destruction of
> our history and loss of natural pursuits. We have viewed rabbits and
> foxes from our school grounds and studied the teeming water-world
> of the adjacent pond, now drained. A new breed of people seem to
> have inhabited the housing estates, dumping rubbish everywhere
> from hedgerows to the local river.'

While the impetus behind this project is a nostalgic regret for what has passed, there is also an intuitive and positive understanding of the need to search for an environmentally acceptable solution where interests clash.

River

The river swirling full of might
Is now reduced to a mere trickle
Among the rusty bedsteads and nails,
The grime, oil and chairs.
It fights to survive,
The brave bold river.

The angry cry of geese
Rings out over
That stretch of oily slick,
No use to anyone.

This is what man has done!
He does not want to care
But Nature cares,
She cares for everything,
Even that trickle
Which was once a shimmering river.

*Simon Robinson 11 years*
*Manor Road County Primary School*
*Chorley, Lancs.*

Rosebery School's anthology was inspired by sycamore and sunflower seeds. Katharine Huggett explains that the original versions were collages and used the actual seeds. In many schools the poems were written as a result of cross-curricular work and here, especially, art and English have combined in an unusual presentation.

Sunflower Seed

Touch me – I am hard and smooth.
Smell me – I have no vapour.
See me – a pear shaped black and white minstrel.
Taste me – nothing!
Listen – mouse silence.

*Emma Rowley 15 years*
*Rosebery School*
*Epsom, Surrey*

Sunflower Seed

lightly grooved nut
marked black and white
stripey snail

oily sheened seed
thin teardropped shape
varnished nail

pointed nosed bead
sleek streamlined fish
badger's head

fossilised stone
dry brittle shell
bone long dead.

*Natasha Shifrin 14 years*
*Rosebery School*
*Epsom, Surrey*

Whitefriars First and Middle School compiled their anthology at a time when their school was threatened with closure. Their teacher, Marion Hammond, explains how this threat of imminent change focused their minds in a very personal way. In a beautifully presented folder the teacher links the sections with her own descriptions of the circumstances in which the poems came to be written. The school has its own 'Wildlife Garden' and here she introduces a section of 'garden' poems.

'The children sat huddled in their anoraks on a dull, drizzly day. Beans and sunflowers had been grown in the summer to provide food to attract wildlife. The remains of these plants looked sad and withered and the pond life was sluggish. We talked about the change of seasons and the children tried to capture the qualities of autumn.'

November Morning

The grass is wet with dew,
The air is filled with dampness.
The sunflower is an old man,
Its face is blank without seeds.
Its back is bending over,
The old man is now a skeleton.

The beans are dead, with their droopy leaves,
The trains pass with their thundery noises,
Seagulls curving in the sky and calling to the sea.

The trees are bare with leaves withering away
    to the ground.
This is a November morning.

*Lok San Liu 11 years*
*Whitefriars First and Middle School*
*Wealdstone, Harrow*


In these few pages it is, of course, impossible to do justice to the vast range of material submitted. The poems in the Appendix beginning on page 86 are a selection of those commended by Ted Hughes. They provide, on the one hand, a tantalising glimpse of the potential for writing in our schools, and, on the other, evidence of children's troubled awareness of the changes taking place in their world.

## 10 The Common Ground

Poetry is in no way élitist. I find more and more that it has as much to offer the less able child as his more able contemporary and can properly form the basis of his language work. The common humanity we share implies a common wavelength of literacy and we should not make the kind of concessions to the less able which exclude them from this wavelength. They must be freed to write well at the level of which they are capable. To achieve this we must dare to apply the same underlying principles; many less able children have a natural affinity with poetry and thus respond well to these. They experience the relief that few words are required, and the security provided by pattern and structure. When listening to poetry they have a deep and natural pleasure in rhyme and rhythm. Moreover, in their writing there is often a refreshing directness and simplicity of expression which a more intelligent child has to struggle to achieve. Often this more 'literary' child's verbal dexterity and more extensive vocabulary create problems of wordiness, turgidity, and metaphors which are contrived and too tightly packed.

Since the introduction of mixed ability English teaching in my school, I have become even more aware of the potential for imaginative writing which is within nearly all children. In her chapter 'The Basics and Remedial English' published in Bernard Harrison's *English Studies 11–18: an arts-based approach*, Bernadette Walsh says this:

> 'It is often held that a remedial secondary pupil must be taught
> "basic" technical skills . . . before more sustained pieces of writing
> can be attempted. It is often held further, that if the pupils cannot
> read fluently in the first place, then what use is it in encouraging
> them to have an interest in literature or to enjoy poetry? If we wish
> the pupils really to possess and use the language, then we must give
> back to them access to their own experience. Only then may we help
> them discover their capacity for art-discourse.'

We deny children this discovery at a tremendous cost. It is no less than to exclude them from our common humanity. Their perceptions are no less fine, their feelings no less complex; their need to express personal experience is certainly no less acute. There is, however, a fine distinction between the kind of frustration which stimulates a positive and excited search for the right words in the right order, and the kind which dispirits and demoralises. There are those children whose grasp of language is so weak that withdrawal into small groups, or even teaching on an individual basis is essential if the wrong kind of frustration is not to develop into alienation. Nevertheless, even these children (two to three percent on average) are able to enjoy poetry and story and to develop the listening ear which is the basis of all language growth. As Bernadette Walsh says, this is to restore to them 'access to their own experience'. When this access is denied, there is no self-acceptance or self-respect. Indeed, a coming to terms with self through literature is a coming to terms with other people and environment.

Before the advent of mixed ability teaching in my school, I found myself at pains to choose 'suitable' poetry for the less able – poetry which was direct, made few linguistic demands and sometimes worked at a lower emotional level. Now, as

I come to write this chapter, I find I have no programme for poetry marked 'for the less able'; they have been engaging at a much higher level and the poetry which I wished to anthologise in this book as representative of the less able has been written within the context of the strategies already outlined. The following poem, for example, was one of these children's attempts to create an 'Impossible Christmas Tree'. He easily understood the abstraction behind the idea. However, he had never heard of the word 'trim' used in this sense; 'Do you mean trim with a pair of scissors?' he asked as he prepared to write. Although he appeared to accept that to 'trim the tree' meant to 'decorate the tree', he clung on to his misunderstanding and turned it into metaphor in an unusual way.

Rainbow Tree

First, I want a beaver to trim the tree
To a sweet, comforting shape.
Then, a rainbow to encircle the tree in its prism of light.
At the top – a carp with its beautiful colours
That reflect in the sun.
Now I need a guard so man cannot harm it –
A lion with a cloudlike mane
And claws like icicles.
Then my tree's beauty is complete
For all to see.

*Lee Clack 12 years*


As an obsessive fisherman, he turned rightly to the roots of his experience, made connections, and wrote well at his own level.

I include this fable by the same child not because it is in any way good writing for a twelve year old but because again it demonstrates a child who has considerable technical difficulties and who does not read easily, nevertheless writing thoughtfully and with a sensitivity which is not lost in the ingenuousness and awkwardness of expression. Moreover, it is 'poetic' – he 'knows' his river in the poetic sense.


River

I walk round Holton Pit with the wind as strong as wood. I see a little boy fishing with all the gear, shouting and splashing in the water. I wonder why he came at all. Then there's an old man, so peaceful, watching his float go up and down. Then, with no warning at all, it shoots along the pit like a frightened rabbit. He plays the fish so gently so as not to hurt it. It comes to the top. It's a carp. Then out comes the landing net. He picks it up with a wet rag, then he slides it back so gently it is as if it were his own child. And there are ducks playing in the reeds so nicely. Then the water shatters as four birds land. And there's a wasp fighting so hard to save himself from drowning. The man finishes. He throws the ducks bread. But all he throws in are lead weights as heavy as death.

*Lee Clack 12 years*


Similarly, the following poems were all written within the context of the work already outlined in previous chapters. I feel they stand well beside the award-winning work written by the average and above average. Above all, they are a justification of a literature-based curriculum for *all* our children.


### Bullfrog

In the river I sit,
on a leaf I stay,
watching the baby
floating down the river,
rocking gently on the shivery water
in the steamy sun.

I wonder why he is on the water.
I wonder why he is in the basket . . .
I wonder why . . .

But still I sit on the water,
on a leaf I stay,
still watching the baby drifting
dreamily away.

*Marie Cantwell 12 years*


### My Dog

My dog is a black bullet,
as sharp as a razor blade.
Its black fur feels soft
as if it had just been woven.
I feel that my dog comforts me.
When I take it for a walk I let it off
and it pants all this slather, a sort of polystyrene.
I call it back. It runs madly towards me.
It jumps on to my chest.
Its pink tongue feels as if it has been dry cleaned.
All the pink bumps on its tongue are sticky.
It feels as if it had just been dry cleaned
because it's so soft and rough.

*Darren Mann 11 years*

## Pigs

If you were to go in a pig shed
ten minutes before feeding time
the innocent-faced pigs
would squeal and jump up
and hang their legs over the side.
Then it would hurt
and they would flop back,
like old rags,
and walk around sniffing
the empty trough.
Then for the full ten minutes
until you had fed them
they would squeal and jump up
and flop back
down again.

If you were to walk in a pen
the squealing would stop
and you would hear quiet grunts
and you would feel a bottle-top nose
pushing at your legs
telling you to hurry up.

Then you could pour in the oats
all over their bottle-top noses.
But they wouldn't care;
they would go on eating
as if there was no more time left in the world.

*Scott Baxter 12 years*


## The Hanging Basket

The hanging basket
Hangs by a single link.
The firmly pressed peat
Holds the imprint of tiny fingers.
Dripping water has made a small puddle
And the reflection of a single red flower;
The splash of the hanging mushroom drip
Falls and dislodges the water,
The flower disappearing into a whirlpool.

*Kevin Gowing 12 years*

## 11 Outlets

The act of writing does not end when the last word is written. The work must be presented. All written work requires this sense of audience (even a 'secret' diary). Somewhere there must be a receiver, somebody who notices what is said and responds. That response is part of the creative experience of the writer and is what we commonly call 'success'. It can happen at various levels and *must* happen if the writer's affirmation of identity within his text is to be confirmed. At the humblest level, this 'success' may be a line, a word, read aloud by the teacher to the child's accepting and appreciative contemporaries. It may be a piece of writing typed and displayed on the wall – the typed word gives a satisfying feeling of importance and recognition. Then, there is the school anthology which can disseminate poetry and story into the local community. As we have already seen, there is the special dimension of the performing arts and, most importantly (because it reaches the widest audience and confirms the sense of identity most wholly), there is publication. It was Herbert Read's vision which first made children's writing accessible to the public at large when he founded what is known today as the W. H. Smith Young Writers' Competition. He believed that while children's writing was necessarily different from adults', it had a special quality of its own and should be read more widely. Today, the word 'competition' is suspect to some. I have found, however, that the excitement of disseminating writing to a wider public fuels the urge to write at all levels of ability. It is so much a matter of putting a high value on children's writing. Yes, some children's work will be selected for publication; others' will not. But the aspiration will be there for all. They will not be false aspirations, either, because all work in which there is genuine involvement and commitment will be valued and made public at one or more of the levels mentioned. Peter Abbs has said.

> 'we want art to penetrate as deeply as it can into both the individual and the community.'

If this is to happen children must engage with the community at both local and national level. We must not patronise them by withdrawing for fear of what we call success or failure. Within a healthy school environment there will be no sense of rejection but rather an underlining of the importance of both the group and the individual. At all costs, we must allow celebration of all art forms. I believe that the arts are in an increasingly beleaguered position in education today. They could be the bedrock of all achievement, including the scientific. In his foreword to *Young Words 1985* (the collection of award winning entries in the W. H. Smith 'Young Writers' competition) Andrew Davies writes:

> 'Teachers these days are belaboured with exhortations to get back to the basics (while going forward into the electronic age), with Philistine notions of relevance to a largely vanished world of mechanical labour, with reductive programmes featuring 'Objectivity', 'Science and Technology' and 'Standards'. The illusory distinction between subjective and objective thinking was exploded long ago, principally by real scientists. The teachers of these fortunate children know that fostering creativity, lateral thinking,

imaginative leaps is not only going to make poems and stories happen. It is keeping alive the kind of innovative thinking that produces breakthroughs in all intellectual fields.'

Certainly, poetry can be the most effective basis for our teaching of English. As the most highly disciplined form of writing, it makes the greatest demands and is a sure path to literacy. It is not enough to put children through certain grammatical hoops on the false assumption that they will emerge literate and competent. This is a soft option which simply does not work. Instead we must return to the richness of our culture and immerse them in its literary forms (as we have seen, reading is an essentially active pursuit when there is true engagement with the text) and then help them to find their own voice within that culture. If successful, we will have a society of people in all walks of life who write clearly and strongly, and who have assimilated correct grammatical forms. They will, of course, also be a thinking people. We must never be traduced by the soft option which neutralises thinking and enervates response.

Butterfly Mania

I am in the tiny world of my creation,
Blossoming from beast to beauty,
I grow to form a picture
Of love and tenderness.

I drip with new born freedom,
I have painted on finest Pierrot silk
The picture of all-seeing eyes,
And formed the liquorice tongue.

I prance and skip over blossoms,
That wait as stepping stones,
I drink their sweet nectar,
Prepared for the gods and then for me.

Life is but a whisper, a flutter of wings,
The swipe of the flexible cage,
With the shining rod of steel, there is no love,
only false beauty, like the smile of a circus clown.

*Stephanie Hayman 15 years*
*Regent's Park School*
*Southampton*
*(Award Winner: 14–16 years)*


Autumn

This is Autumn,
A flyaway animal,
A speechless creature
Found in a world of woods;
Abandoned by summer,
It moults in a turn of the year;
It bites with blunt teeth.
Its colours:
Crimson, yellow, grey and green
Were collected
Through the years:
The yellow from the burning summer sun,
The grey from winter skies,
The green from fresh spring grass,
The crimson from forgotten fires.

A fearless animal,
Lost and then found.

It feeds on Sunday strolls.

Please leave the peace unbroken.

*Heidi Masters 11 years*
*Halesworth Middle School*
*Halesworth, Suffolk*


Winter

Four figures – I saw them
Four figures – I'm sure.
Four figures – silent
Four figures – powerful.

Young Boy-Winter likes to play pranks.
He draws on windows and sprays stolen snow on
     walls and fences.
He's quiet and timid.

Old Man-Winter sprawls on the ground
Leaving all his prints to be found.
But he's never to be seen.
He's always invisible.

Mrs. Winter lets the tide roam far and wide.
Makes you wish you'd stayed at home.
With her rolling pin she whirls,
Wanting you to go home.

Mr. Winter goes stampeding, destroying, racing himself.
Booming, blustering, clashing, roaring, whirling around.
Fuming, eating up branches with fury and anger,
Roaring anger takes him on.

*Toby Frost 7 years*
*Beechwood Park Junior School*
*Markyate, Herts.*


'No Fishing'

'No Fishing' the sign read
In big bold black capitals.
'No Fishing!' yelled the gamekeeper, when he saw us
Brandishing our puny little rods
And our tins full of worms.
We never did fish there.
Instead, we hid away in the bracken –
Watching and waiting . . .

We watched the trout glide through the ferny reeds
And voles as they scurried through the
    undergrowth.
We were charmed by the dragonflies
Skimming the surface, like dainty ballerinas.

Then we saw the kingfisher.
His turquoise plumage flashed like some rare gem.
A streak of sunlight . . .
    A ripple of reflections . . .
        Then he reappeared.
Clasped in his beak, a sliver of silver stars.
'No Fishing' we said.

*Mhairi O'Neil 15 years*
*Dollar Academy*


The Waterfall

People thought you were safe and beautiful
But then they saw you swallow up the world,
All of it,
Whole.
Smashing it up,
Engulfing every living thing
Until you had finished
Leaving only yourself
Standing there in the universe.
The only beautiful object
In an everlasting space
Drawing in knowledge of other planets
Until you were alone
Satisfied yet guilty.

*Jessica Leff 11 years*
*Fitzjohn's Primary School*
*London*


'If You Find a Dead Bird Anywhere . . .

On the news the other night,
It showed pictures of the plight of swans
With feathers so matted with oil
They couldn't move,
And soon they died.

Their lifeless bodies unrecognisable,
Looking more like brown round boulders
Sticking up out of the river.

*Angela Powell*
*Llansamlet Junior Comprehensive*
*Swansea*

Invasion

Emptiness, a shadow,
That's now disappearing,
for,
Mud is all around looking like
A top of a melting digestive biscuit.
Tubing is a monster's secret hideaway
From the buildings which are
Giant space ships
Transformed into dolls' houses.
The cars all around us are
Tamed robots,
Spies for a distant planet.

*Philippa Johnstone 12 years*
*The Crestwood School*
*Eastleigh, Hants.*

The Estate

The estate is quiet on the windy morning,
Bottles clatter noisily down steps
And along alleyways,
Papers blotched with grease
Dancing grey depressing dances.

Broken windows glitter like spider webs,
Everyone catching the sunlight,
Catching your eye,
Graffiti splotched untidily on a wall,
Left by a careless hand
Which didn't care.
Who would have the energy to
On this awful estate?

In one of the flats a couple
Starts to get drunk.
Their baby squawls.
He wants feeding.

He's seriously ill.
'Shut up!'
The father yells drunkardly,
And he gets up,
Goes to the baby's room
And hits it.
The baby, all of a sudden,
Stops.

And suddenly all around the flat,
The father hears the wind cursing him.

*Giovanna Lozzi*
*Trinity High School*
*Woodford Green*


Kestrel

The kestrel swoops along the motorways,
Picking at the corpses
Killed by cars whizzing along
All day, and all night
At just over 70 mph.

Free from jurisdiction
The kestrel goes and does where it pleases.
On good days a mouse, or a hedgehog maybe;
And on bad, simply
Fresh wind and free flight.

*Peter Grant*
*Maxwelltown High School*
*Dumfries.*


My Field (an extract)

The fieldmouse speaks:
The stubble burns.
As I watch from a hedge,
Dragonflies of ash float up as if from water,
Then . . . a short life fails and they die back down.
Fish of flame dance on the black water,
Eating at the golden leftovers,
And the red crabs move past
Slowly.
Black,
Creeping, stalking,
Soaking into the golden brown.

A sturdy stalk melts down to a delicate powder
As a black carpet rises, then falls.
My field has shed his summer clothes,
His winter coat dark.
The world I love
Is gone.

*Lara Mair 10 years*
*Halesworth Middle School*
*Halesworth, Suffolk*


We Are the Heavies

We are the heavies, the heavies, the heavies
We are the metals mercury and lead,
We build up in organs
And build up in tissues
We travel through food chains
And poison the brain.

We are the pesticides, pesticides, pesticides,
We poison the air
And we poison the sea,
We are the aldrin, the dieldrin, the gases
We are the pesticides
LET US BE FREE.

Puny men spray us
Control us they think.
But we are the strength
Not they, not they.
We kill all of NATURE
Ending in man
We are the heavies, the heavies, the heavies
Now LET US BE FREE.

*John Grace 13 years*
*Llansamlet Junior Comprehensive*
*Swansea*


Fox Hunt

'A fine day for it.'
(The sky is as blue as blood).
'A slight nip in the air,
One could be in for a killing.'

Herod's horn is blown.

The frightened fox escapes the cage.
At last freedom . . .
On a leash.

Heavy thuds of horses' hooves
And howling bites the air.
The little dart is running red
And effort strains his watery eyes.

Later, back in the cherry-lit bar,
The redcoats boast and drink a toast
To prosperity and a long life.

*Marcus Beasley 15 years*
*East Hampstead Park School*
*Wokingham, Berks*


Grey Squirrel

The grey squirrel is sharp
On the move.
He smells of the inside of a tree
Woody.

*Peter Gregory 13 years*
*Llansamlet Junior Comprehensive*
*Swansea*


The Killers

Juggernauts rushing by,
Killers spitting grit and dust,
The smell of fumes
Strangling the rich clean air
All on the Rochester Way.

Factories smoking along the side
With murky black smoke confusing the traffic
All on the Rochester Way.

One little wet-the-bed stands on its own
Pushing its way through the pavement
Trying to find a new way of life
All on the Rochester Way.

*Michelle Casserly 9 years*
*St Thomas More Primary School*
*London*

The Bold Eagle

All the long night and all the long day
He sits on his perch
The Golden Eagle, exhibit No. 7.
DO NOT FEED THIS ANIMAL.
Sometimes he shifts,
Gliding through the air
Like a clipped goose,
From one perch to the other;
His huge talons grip the stand majestically,
But his legs are bandy and his wobbly knees
    tremble and shake.

Dinner time!
The juicy meat flies into his old withered cage,
His sharp beak jabbing it until there's nothing left:
Nothing but screaming sticky children,
And the memory of free flight through
Wide windy spaces;
High over trees and jagged cliffs
Until tea time.

*Andrew Finnie 12 years*
*Maxwelltown High School*
*Dumfries*

Building

From our classroom windows
We once saw as far as the sea,
The hares fighting in the field,
The children playing on the tree swing.

From our classroom windows
We once saw the sunset in the sky,
The Ribble estuary sparkling in the sunlight,
The ponds and the trees.

Now from our classroom windows
We see the buildings,
The bedroom windows,
The washing lines.

Now from our classroom windows
We see the sheds,

The greenhouses,
And the drain pipes.

*Stephen Worbey 11 years*
*Manor Road County Primary School*
*Chorley, Lancs.*


Walking the Fields

The iced fields were like a gigantic Christmas cake,
Trees were decorations,
My pony just a plastic figure.
I opened the frozen gate; my hand stuck to the clasp,
    metal on magnet.
Birds clung to the wire, frozen stiff.
My footprints were like a monster's feet in cement.
I walked further – nothing more than a cushion of mohair.
It was all a 3D picture.
I patted my plastic pony.

I turned to go and looked at this unreal world.
As I walked back across the gigantic Christmas cake,
The surface cracked like crispy bacon rind,
Sun broke out from the clouds,
Unreal returned to real.

*Sarah Wright 12 years*
*Halesworth Middle School*
*Halesworth, Suffolk*


For the Want of Power

N ever ending battles used to be talked about.
U nluckily for humanity technology enveloped us.
C lever scientists thought of all save the
L asting effects of a five minute brawl,
E verlasting death to follow.
A h but you are thinking there has been no war.
R emember those clever scientists?
W anting to show off their toys,
A greed on a test zone.
R egarded an area with greatest care and,
D ropped big bombs on it.
E ternal sadness enveloped the land.
S o the innocent birds are gone
T o a much better place but who cares.
R ich and wealthy, the scientists sip martinis.

O ver dinner they talk of what they have done.
Y et certain countries only think of the power
S tockpiling the world's history.
A ll the leaders say it's only defence, but,
L ying behind Greenham's fences a
L ast chapter is waiting to be written.

*Michael Bathurst  13 years*
*France Hill School*
*Camberley, Surrey*


## The Red Bus Chugs

The red bus chugs.
 The squirrel hides.
The crane cranks.
 The squirrel climbs.
The taxi paps.
 The squirrel wanders.
The motorbike roars.
 The squirrel ponders.
The tractor churns.
 The squirrel skips.
The train blares.
 The squirrel turns.
The lorry lumbers.
 The squirrel runs.
The car brakes.
 The squirrel sprawls.
The bulldozer clangs.
 The squirrel dies.
But the red bus chugs.

*Zoe Roscoe  13 years*
*Riverway C. of E. Middle School*
*Stafford*


## The Death Sentence

Tall straight pillars,
Huge great trees,
Large maybe
But defenceless,
Like children,
Deserted by parents.

The axe swings,
The tree falls,
As a soldier in battle.
But the tree has no mouth
To protest.
The tree has no legs
To run.
The tree has no gun
To take revenge.
For the sake of a table;
A sheet of paper;
A cabinet;
Trees
Standing tall and dark
Large and menacing
But defenceless against
The lumberjack's axe.
One by one they fall
As soldiers in the battle.
A forest full of life,
Then nothing.

*Briony Verdon  12 years*
*Codsall Middle School*
*Wolverhampton*

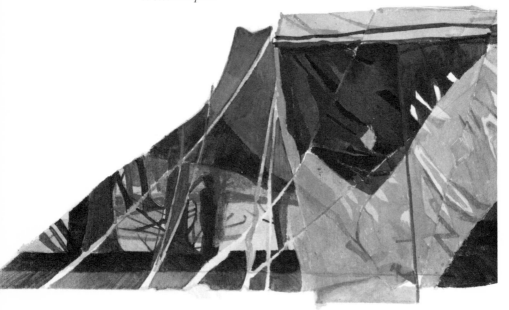

# References

ABBS, PETER (1982) *English Within the Arts* (Hodder and Stoughton)

BROWNJOHN, SANDY (1982) *What Rhymes With Secret?* (Hodder and Stoughton)

CHURCH, RICHARD (1955) *Over the Bridge* (Heinemann)

CROSSLEY-HOLLAND, KEVIN (1965) *The Battle of Maldon and other Old English Poems* (Macmillan)

DAVIES, ANDREW (1986) Foreword to *Young Words 1985* (Macmillan)

FAIRFAX, JOHN; MOAT, JOHN (1981) *The Way to Write* (Elm Tree Books/Hamish Hamilton)

GORDON, JOHN (1975) 'On Firm Ground'; essay in *The Thorny Paradise* ed. Edward Blishen (Kestrel Books)

HEANEY, SEAMUS (1980) *Selected Poems 1965–75* (Faber)

HINES, BARRY (1968) *A Kestrel for a Knave* (Penguin)

HUGHES, TED (1967) *Poetry in the Making* (Faber)

HUGHES, TED (1984) *What Is The Truth?* (Faber)

LEE, LAURIE (1969) *Cider With Rosie* (The Hogarth Press)

LE GUIN, URSULA (1973) *A Wizard of Earthsea* (Victor Gollancz)

LE GUIN, URSULA (1973) *Dreams Must Explain Themselves* (Algol; reprinted in *Signal 19*, 1976)

LE GUIN, URSULA (1975) 'This Fear of Dragons' essay in *The Thorny Paradise* ed. Edward Blishen (Kestrel Books)

SANDERS, GEORGE (1971) *I Took My Mind A Walk* (Penguin English Stage One)

TANNER, HEATHER AND ROBIN (1981) *Woodland Plants* (Robin Garton Ltd)

WALSH, BERNADETTE (1983) 'The Basics and Remedial English'; chapter 4 in *English Studies 11–18: an arts-based approach*, ed. HARRISON, BERNARD (Hodder and Stoughton)

# Acknowledgments

We are grateful for permission to reproduce the following material: to W. H. Smith Ltd for 'The Dog' Andrew Holmes (Award Winner Young Writers' Competition 1982. Published in *Young Writers 24th Year* 1983); 'Trying to Unblock a Drain in Winter' Ian Self (Award Winner Young Writers' Competition 1982. Published in *Young Writers 24th Year* 1983); 'The Making of a Hornet' Rachel Harrison (Award Winner Young Writers' Competition 1984. Published in *Young Writers 26th Year* 1985); 'The Christmas Scene: Through The Eyes of an Artist' and 'Heath Groundsel' Kay Chambers (Award Winner Young Writers' Competition 1984, Published in *Young Writers 26th Year* 1985); 'Ploughing' Trevor Guyton (Award Winner Young Writers' Competition 1984. Published in *Young Writers 26th Year* 1985); 'Gran', 'Dancing Butterflies' and 'The Thought Bird' Gregory Block (Runner-up in Young Writers' Competition 1984. Published in *Young Writers 26th Year* 1985); 'Pig' Lucy Gardner (Award Winner Young Writers' Competition 1985. Published in *Young Words 1986*); 'The Starling's Truth' Andrew Farrow (Award Winner Young Writers' Competiton 1985. Published in *Young Words 1986*); 'Old Grandma', 'Leaving of Swallows' and 'A Fish' Gail Bloomfield (Special Award Winner Young Writers' Competition 1986. Published in *Young Words 1987*); 'Mole' Joseph Frost (Award Winner Young Writers' Competition 1986. Published in *Young Words 1987*); 'Senses' Ruth Kingshott (Award Winner Young Writers' Competition 1986 Published in *Young Words 1987*); 'Pheasant Chick' Caroline English (Award Winner Young Writers' Competition 1986. Published in *Young Words 1987*); 'A Boxer Dog' Sally Clifton (Award Winner Young Writers' Competition 1986. Published in *Young Words 1987*); 'Morning Cow' Darren Pearce (Award Winner Young Writers' Competition 1986. Published in *Young Words 1987*); 'The Badger' Jamie MacDonald (Award Winner Young Writers' Competition 1986. Published in *Young Words 1987*); 'The Silver Catfish' Lara Mair (Award Winner Young Writers' Competition 1986. Published in *Young Words 1987*); 'Four Rabbit Kittens Stare' Stephen Goodwin (Runner-up in Young Writers' Competition 1986. Published in *Young Words 1987*); 'The Truth of a Rabbit' Malcolm Goodwin (Runner-up in Young Writers' Competition 1986. Published in *Young Words 1987*). To the *Observer* for 'Noah's Ark' Emma Smith 1st in 11–14 years section, Observer Children's National Poetry Writing Competition. Published 21.9.86.; 'The Terrapin' Matthew Shepherd Runner-up in 11–14 years section. Published 21.9.86.; 'River Blyth' Matthew Watson; 'Tree Collection' Lara Mair; 'Fate' Caroline English; 'That Pond!' Rosalind Roberts; 'Our Pond' Russell Wood; 'Noah's Ark' Sarah Wright; 'The Ark' Charlotte Hawthorn; 'Seaside Show' Ruth Hooton; 'The Great Flood' Gail Bloomfield; 'Washed Up' Matthew Goddard; 'The River' Malcolm Goodwin; published 28.9.86. The author would particularly like to thank all those children of Halesworth Middle School, past and present, whose writings have given so much pleasure to so many.